ABOUT THE BOOK

This book is a practical and holistic step-by-step guide to homebuying, which is told through the author's personal experiences. It is intended to be a to-the-point and no-nonsense guide, written in simple language and in an easy to follow approach that will provide you, the reader, a straight forward map on how to get your feet on the property ladder or grow your property portfolio.

The information provided is based on a simple framework, which you can memorise through the expression:

Buddy Let's Plan For Action.

The following key aspects are covered within this framework:

1. **Believe** — believe that you can purchase property and grow your wealth through your purchase.
2. **Learn** — learn about the real estate market and how to make money from it.
3. **Plan** — plan your purchase so you can get the highest return out of your investment.
4. **Fund** — raise the money through your own equity and through loans from banks and other sources to help you purchase property.
5. **Act** — find, buy, manage and eventually sell your property for a profit

I promise that if you follow the steps outlined in this book, you will not only get on the property ladder but will also set yourself up for financial success.

Dedicated to my late father,

the most generous person I have ever known or met.

"A QUITTER NEVER WINS, A WINNER NEVER QUITS"

-Napoleon Hill

PREFACE

WHY THIS BOOK?

Hardly a day goes by where there are no reports in the media detailing how costly property has become in cities such as London, Sydney, Auckland and Vancouver — and how hard it is for aspiring home owners, especially millennials, to even get on the property ladder. I, therefore, thought, *What better way to give back to society than to help first time buyers get on the property ladder in such an unfavourable climate by sharing my and other successful property investors' knowledge and experience?* You should find this book equally helpful if you are already a property owner and want to grow your portfolio.

To give you a sense of the struggle that first time property buyers are facing, Apartment List's survey of 24,000 apartment renters found that 80% of millennial renters want to purchase a property but are unable to afford that property. Some millennials may be facing a wait of over two decades before they can afford to buy a property!

As I write this book, property prices have very recently softened in major cities such as Sydney and Auckland — due to government efforts to curb price growth — and in London due to the uncertainty caused by Brexit. If this is still the situation while you read this book and you are a first-time buyer, then it may just be the perfect time for you to purchase your first property in those locations!

You may ask why you should read this book when there are many other real estate investment books out there. I have read tens of books on real estate and often continue to read new ones. I always find that every time I read a new book, firstly it refreshes my memory on key concepts and best practices, and secondly, I often find a few very useful new tips that I have never come across before. What makes this book different is that it tackles the problem in a very pragmatic manner and includes softer, more human aspects; e.g. truly believing that you can achieve something – which are critical in achieving success in any endeavour, but especially in purchasing real estate!

This book incorporates my personal experiences investing in properties, my work as a successful professional, and it also includes some of the critical life lessons I have learned along the way that have helped me achieve success. My hope is that they will help you, as well.

Most of the property data and examples I have used are from the US, New Zealand, Australia and the UK. I have also done a deep dive into the New Zealand residential market as a case study, as it has had some of the highest property price growths in the past few years but properties in several of its cities have become overpriced. Millennials and post-millennials in New Zealand are amongst those who most feel the pinch in buying their first property. The property situation in New Zealand serves as a good reason for you to do a deeper study of the property market in your own country and city prior to beginning your property quest. Similar, broader principles will apply regardless of where you invest.

I am from Generation X and was fortunate enough to buy my first property in the early 2000s. However, it was not smooth sailing at that time either, and I was very lucky to meet smart investors who steered me from the path of what I call 'disbelief and debt' and onto that of 'believing and investing'.

I have tried to explain as much of my personal experience as possible so you have a practical, real-world example of how one can overcome bad financial habits, laziness and lack of belief to develop the right mindset as an investor. I also provide examples of others who have succeeded, in some cases, far beyond my own accomplishments. I have, however, focused on the examples of those who are everyday people — like you and me (rather than the super-rich or Ultra High Net-Worth Individuals) so you can realise and believe that anyone can own property and build a portfolio.

There are some more technical sections in the book, but I have clearly highlighted these as optional reads for readers who want to gain a deeper understanding of certain concepts. There are also some charts and tables, but I have tried to keep these as simple as possible and you should find them useful and easy to follow.

There are those people who talk and complain and there are those who *do*. If you are reading this book, then I would bet money that you fall into the latter category.

I sincerely hope that you will find this book helpful and will get value out of it.

THE SPIRAL FAN CARD DECK TRICK AND THE MAGIC OF LEARNING

While I was in Brazil, a friend once performed a card trick that left me baffled. He took a normal deck of cards and turned with his back to me for a couple of minutes and — voila — he ended up with the below design:

I simply could not understand how he managed to produce this formation in a matter of minutes. I thought he may have been hiding another deck somewhere but even if that was the case, I still wondered how he would have gotten that perfect design. Unfortunately, this was before the days of Google, so I could not simply jump online and find out his secret.

It took me a few days to convince my friend to show me how he performed the trick. The process is actually very simple:

1. Start with a standard deck with all cards perfectly stacked.
2. Firmly hold the top left corner with your left thumb and index finger.

3. Then, with your right thumb and index finger, apply pressure to the bottom right corner but almost as if you are very slightly spreading the corner out.
4. Then very gently rotate the deck so that the top left corner now becomes the bottom right corner and repeat step 3.
5. Repeat step 4 until you have a perfect fan!
6. You can subtly change the shape of the fan by applying more pressure on one corner.

If the above instructions are a bit difficult to follow, simply google 'spiral fan card deck trick' and you will find a number of videos that guide you through the process.

You might be wondering why I am talking about this card trick in a book that is supposed to be about buying property. You are not alone — my wife thought I had lost the plot and asked the same question when she read the first draft!

There is a key objective for this. Sometimes a task, such as buying a property, can look very complex and you may think you are incapable of accomplishing it. You may also think that only certain people with special skills or capabilities can do it. However, often if you learn how to do something properly, you realise that the task was not so complex after all. There are simply three key things here:

1. Believing you can achieve the task,
2. Learning how to do it, and
3. Practicing and *doing* it!

THE KEY PRINCIPLES OF THIS BOOK

As a consultant I was taught to always use frameworks to analyse and solve problems, and so I thought it would be useful to present you with a simple framework to solve the little problem of getting on the property ladder and growing your portfolio.

There are a few basic principles that this book is based on and all the other details are woven around these. The BUDDY LETS PLAN FOR ACTION framework below highlights these key concepts:

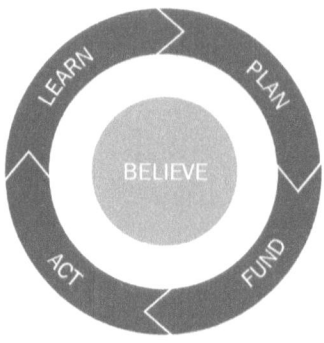

Step 1 - The underlying concept of this book is to **BELIEVE**. If you believe, then you can achieve whatever you want! And to believe you must have a clear image of what you wish to accomplish.

Step 2 is to **LEARN**, i.e. to deeply get to know and understand the real estate industry and the market(s) in which you want to buy property. This book gives an overview of what real estate is and how it is valued. It also covers information on some of the high-growth residential real estate markets.

Step 3 is to **PLAN** how you will achieve your goals. You need a short-term plan, a mid-term plan and a long-term plan. You will also need to constantly review and fine-tune your plan.

Step 4 is to **FUND** your investment by saving and raising money through other avenues in order to acquire your investments. The book describes a number of avenues in which you can raise money for your investments, both through equity (i.e. your own capital) and loans.

Step 5 is to then **ACT**! This includes finding the best properties to acquire, acquiring these properties and managing them. The last part of this step is to have an exit strategy and actioning it.

Whilst some of the steps have dedicated chapters, the overall principles are interwoven throughout this book.

NAVIGATING THE BOOK

This book has 4 sections as follows:

- **Section A** focuses on Step 2 (learning)
- **Sections B and C** focus on Steps 3 to 5 (planning, funding and acting)
- **Section D** covers Step 1 (believing) and further aspects of Step 2 (learning)

If you are familiar with the fundamentals of real estate feel free to either skim read or skip Section A and use it for reference if required.

SECTION A - OVERVIEW OF REAL ESTATE

"Live as if you were to die tomorrow. Learn as if you were to live forever."

-Mahatma Gandhi

CHAPTER 1: WHAT REAL ESTATE IS AND WHY BUY OR INVEST IN PROPERTY

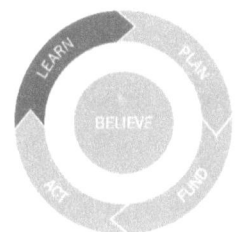

WHAT IS REAL ESTATE?

Let us start by defining "real estate" or "property" (I use these words interchangeably).

According to Investopedia.com:

"Real estate is property comprised of land, the buildings on it as well as the natural resources of the land including uncultivated flora and fauna, farmed crops and livestock, water and minerals."

According to businessdictionary.com Real estate means:

"Land and anything fixed, immovable, or permanently attached to it such as appurtenances, buildings, fences, fixtures, improvements, roads, shrubs and trees (but not growing crops), sewers, structures, utility systems, and walls. Title to real estate normally includes title to air rights, mineral rights, and surface rights which can be bought, leased, sold, or transferred together or separately. Also called real property or realty."

In the spirit of keeping things simple, you can think of residential real estate as; **the land and the buildings on that land.**

WHY BUY OR INVEST IN PROPERTY?

When I told one of my good friends about this book and potentially investing together in the future, he said something which I really liked:

'Real estate is the ultimate parking lot for money' — Lerang Selolwane, CEO, Mining Engineering Company, Botswana

I am sure hardly anyone would argue with this statement.

There are numerous reasons to invest in property. Below I have highlighted some of those key reasons:

1. A PHYSICAL, TANGIBLE ASSET

A major advantage of investing in property is that it is a physical, tangible asset that you directly control. It is not like owning shares, which are *indirectly* linked to tangible assets and generally belong to a public company over which you have no say.

2. LIMITED SUPPLY AND POTENTIAL CAPITAL GAINS

Simply put, at this stage we only know of one habitable planet — our planet earth — and that is unlikely to change for a little while! Economics is all about supply and demand. We have a simple equation here — the world's population is increasing and there is an increasing middle class who can afford property; however, the quantity of land (in particular, *desirable* land or space) is static. In fact, the amount of available land will most likely reduce with rising sea levels in the coming decades! Hence economics dictates that on average, in the long term, the price of land (a proxy for property) will continue to rise.

If we look at overall New Zealand prices as an example (see chart below), the value multiplied by 5 in the past 25 years and increased by over 60% in the past 5 years. Other markets, such as Canada, Britain and Australia, have also seen not too dissimilar trajectories.

Figure 1: HOUSE PRICE INDEX - SELECT COUNTRIES - 1980 TO 2016 (Global House Prices - The Economist, 2017)

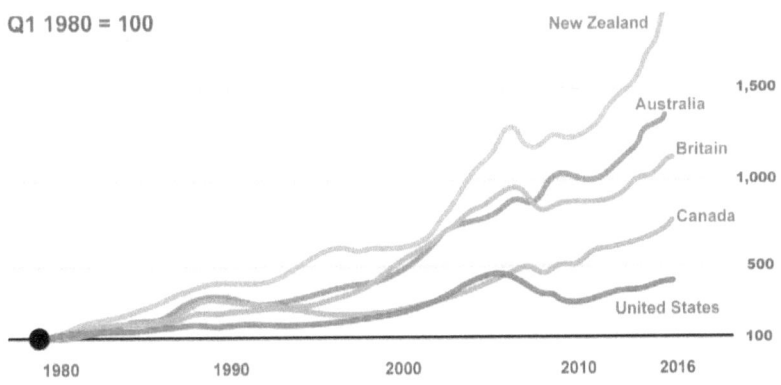

The chart below shows the property price growth for a number of other countries and — barring a few exceptions — most countries have seen substantial price growth in the past twenty years.

Figure 2: HOUSE PRICE INDEX - SELECT COUNTRIES - 1997 TO 2016 (Business Insider Australia, 2015)

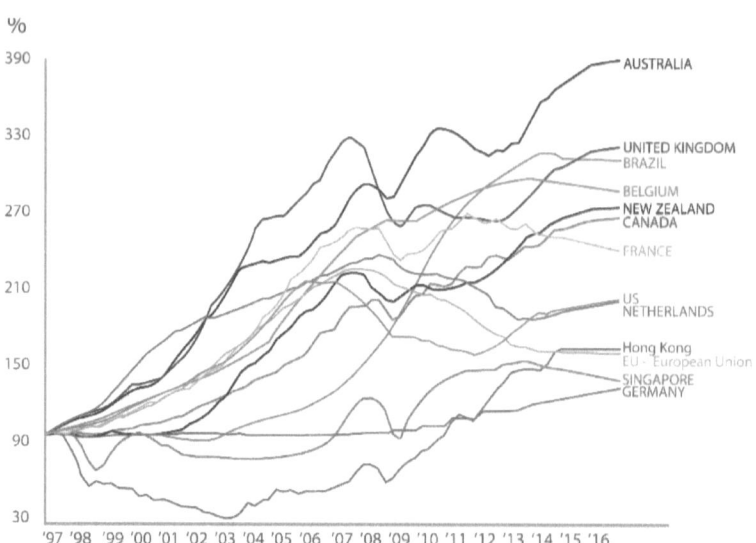

To this end, **as a long-term investment,** property investment can give very good returns, provided, as in the case of any investment, you do your homework and choose the right investment (right property, right location and right time).

CAUTION - In the chart above, you will also notice that in the short run, property values can drop. Therefore you should always have a long-term investment horizon for properties, as you could lose substantial money if you invest on a short-term basis and the market turns. You will also note that I have stressed that you must do your homework and find the right investment. You will find much more detail on this later.

3. A BALANCED RISK/RETURN PROFILE COMPARED TO OTHER INVESTMENT CLASSES

For a non-institutional or non-professional investor, some of the key investment options are as below:

Figure 3: TABLE OF RISK VS. RETURN FOR DIFFERENT ASSET CLASSES

TYPE OF INVESTMENT	RETURN	RISK
Savings accounts or government bonds	LOW	LOW
Shares (equities) in publicly traded companies	HIGH	HIGH
Real estate	MEDIUM	MEDIUM
Other (e.g. paintings, vintage cars, wines, etc.)	HIGH	HIGH

Figure 4: RISK VS. RETURN CHART FOR DIFFERENT ASSET CLASSES

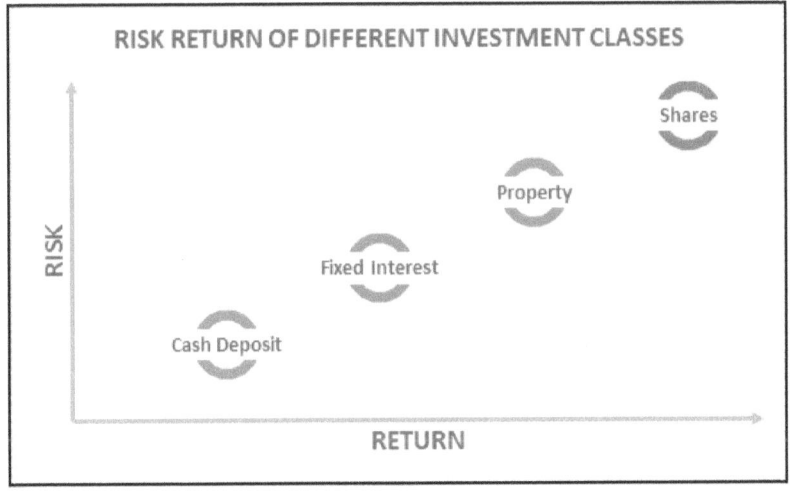

The risk/return profile of real estate is between investing in savings accounts or government bonds and equities, or other types of exotic investments.

Real estate prices generally rise and fall slower than equities and bonds, thus protecting you from volatility (variability) of values.

Looking at the returns of different asset classes in Australia in the chart below, we observe that residential property gave the same returns as shares but with a lot less volatility. High returns with low volatility is exactly what every investor wants!

However, I am not telling you to put all your eggs in one basket by only investing in property – consider the risk/return profile when you make any investment decisions and ensure that you are optimising those investments through a balanced portfolio.

Figure 5: RETURNS OF DIFFERENT ASSET CLASSES IN AUSTRALIA – 1926 to 2006 (New Haven R.E)

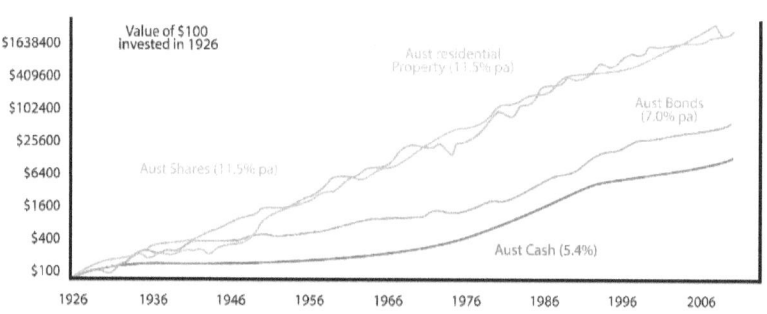

Sources: ABS, REIA, Global Financial Data, AMP Capital Investors.

4. CONSISTENT PERFORMANCE

As you can see from the chart in Point 3 above, real estate can give consistent performance year after year. Whilst there can be a few dips here and there, the overall volatility compared to the shares market is much lower and the overall trend has generally been upwards.

5. THE POWER OF LEVERAGE (OR GOOD DEBT)

Banks will only lend a large percentage of the investment amount (up to 100% or even higher in some cases) to individuals for the purchase of real estate. There is no other investment class for which banks will risk giving high leverage to an individual. Additionally, the cost of borrowing is typically far less for property than for other investment classes such as shares.

Now let us look at why this is so important. It all comes down to what we call **the power of leverage**.

Let us say that a bank lends you 80% of the value for the purchase of a house worth $600,000. This means that you will put a down payment of $120,000 (i.e. 20% of the total value). Now consider that the property value goes up by 5% in one year. What will your return be? It will be much higher that what you may be thinking. Let us go through the computation:

- Initial value = $600,000
- New value = 1.05 * $600,000 = $630,000
- Value increase = $30,000
- Your initial investment = $120,000
- Return on investment in one year = $30,000 / $120,000 = 25%

In other words, you made a return of 25% despite the property value only growing by 5%.

This is the power of leverage. And you could only benefit to this extent as a non-institutional investor when you purchase real estate. While you may accumulate debt to purchase other forms of investments, the percentage of leverage you obtain will be far less than in the case of real estate and the cost of the debt (i.e. interest) will be much higher.

You may also believe that debt is supposed to be bad and that we should always avoid it. Is that not what our parents taught us? If you are going to borrow money to buy a car or another household item, then I fully agree that debt is bad. Firstly, it is expensive; secondly it begs the question as to whether you could really afford the item you bought if you had to borrow money for it. However, when debt is used to acquire a sound and well thought-out investment, it can be a very powerful tool in raising capital so that you can acquire the asset in the first place. Secondly, it greatly enhances your returns. Here is another example of this:

Imagine you already have a house that you have fully paid off. Let's say it is worth $500,000. If the property value goes up by 10% then you make $50,000.

Now consider that situation where you re-mortgage your house and buy another house for $500,000.

- Total assets = $500,000 + $500,000 = $1,000,000
- Debt = $500,000
- Equity = $500,000
- Let's assume that the interest rate you pay is 5%, hence the interest amount paid for one year is $25,000.
- Now let's take the same scenario where the property value goes up by 10%. The total value of your assets went up by 10% * $1,000,000 = $100,000
- Cost of debt (interest) for the year = $25,000
- Net return = $75,000

Hence you are $25,000 better off in this simplified scenario because of the power of leverage.

6. ABILITY TO BORROW MORE IF INVESTMENT VALUE RISES

If the value of your investment or home rises, you could use your asset to borrow more from the bank, e.g. to raise equity for another investment or for any other reason you need the cash, such as paying for education. The idea would be to spend the released cash in a sensible manner so you do not over leverage yourself for no reason.

I have consistently used equity in my existing properties to buy additional properties, particularly as property prices have increased over the past few years. To give you a specific example, within a year of buying my first property, its value went up by over 20% due firstly to the very good price I paid for it, secondly; the improvements I made to it, and lastly; the property price growth during that period. I ended up with about $40,000 of equity, which I then used to finance the purchase of my next property. At that time the banks allowed me to get away with an overall borrowing of 90%.

Property prices continued to climb after my second purchase and I continued to use the additional equity with other savings to finance new purchases.

7. ABILITY TO IMPROVE THE VALUE OF THE ASSET

As property is a physical, tangible asset that you directly control, you can make improvements to increase the value of the asset. This is not the case for other investment classes such as shares. The ability to improve the value can have huge benefits as it not only increases the value of the asset but can also increase the income you receive *from* your asset.

I recently added a new room to one of my existing properties. This increased its weekly rent by $50 and added over $50,000 (possibly as much as $100,000) to its value, and all I had to spend was a little over $20,000. That is a return of 13% on the investment of the $20,000 (i.e. $50 x 52 / $20,000 = 13%).

Clearly not all investments will yield this kind of return but there is potential value to be added if you critically assess your asset and do your homework on the best way to optimise its value. You also must be careful to not end up wasting money, e.g. doing a lavish upgrade of a kitchen in your rental property may make the house look very nice but may not necessarily give you a positive return in the long term. Of course, if you have the money to splash and want to upgrade certain parts of your own home regardless of the return, then your comfort takes priority over the returns.

8. UPFRONT INCOME

If you are buying property for investment, then you will find that there are hardly any investments where you get your income upfront and pay expenses later (i.e. have negative working capital). Let us expand on this a bit more: imagine you have a small corner store as a business. You will need to pay upfront rent for your premises, pay for the goods (e.g. groceries) you are going to sell and then eventually make money. If you buy shares in a company, you will only get returns at the end of the year if there are dividends declared. In property, on the other hand, you get your rental income upfront — at the beginning of each monthly or weekly cycle — yet you pay your mortgage at the end of the month. In essence you have negative working capital, which is a very good position to be in!

9. INFLATION-PROOF INVESTMENT CLASS

Another key advantage of real estate is that it is an inflation-proof investment class. On average, the cost of rent will rise with inflation. If you are renting out your property, your rent will generally go up with inflation thus protecting your future returns.

10. PASSIVE INCOME

According to Investopedia, passive income is the earning an individual derives from a rental property, limited partnership or other enterprise in which he or she is not materially involved.

Passive income is what we are all looking for, because passive income enables you to maintain an income month after month without doing any extra work. Rental property can provide this if it is a good investment and you have it managed by a professional property manager.

My personal objective of building up my property portfolio is to have passive income to complement my earnings from working as a professional and to eventually use this income for retirement.

11. POTENTIAL TAX SAVINGS THROUGH GEARING

Many countries (including the US, New Zealand, Australia and the UK at the time of writing this book) allow interest on your mortgage on a buy-to-let property to offset your overall taxes. There are special rules in each country on the extent to which you can offset the taxes.

For countries allowing full tax-offsetting, let us take a simple example as follows:

- Net rental income after all expenses: $15,000

- 5% Interest on mortgage of $200,000 = $10,000
- You pay tax on $15,000 - $10,000 = $5,000 (instead of paying tax on the whole net rental value of $15,000)
- If your marginal tax rate (i.e. the tax rate for the top tax bracket of your income) is 40% then you pay $2,000 (instead of $6,000 if you had to pay on the whole net rental amount)

CHANGES TO BE AWARE OF IN THE UK

The UK has recently changed the tax offsetting rules for buy-to-let properties. According to the UK HM Revenues and Customs website (www.gov.uk, 2017):

Landlords will be able to obtain relief as follows:

- in 2017 to 2018 the deduction from property income (as is currently allowed) will be restricted to 75% of finance costs, with the remaining 25% being available as a basic rate tax reduction *(the basic tax rate was 20% at the time of the writing of this book)*
- in 2018 to 2019, 50% finance costs deduction and 50% given as a basic rate tax reduction
- in 2019 to 2020, 25% finance costs deduction and 75% given as a basic rate tax reduction
- from 2020 to 2021 all financing costs incurred by a landlord will be given as a basic rate tax reduction

If your marginal tax on your rental revenue is higher than the basic tax rate, then you will not be better or worse off. However, if your marginal tax rate is higher than the basic rate, you will get less tax savings.

Donald Trump's recent US tax changes (based on the Tax Cuts and Jobs Act passed in December 2017) have many upsides but tax deductions as a result of mortgages will see a drop. According to Mansion Global (Hendrickson, 2018), the deduction for mortgage interest will be limited to loans of up to $750,000, or $375,000 for married couples filing separately. The upper limit was previously $1 million. This cap only affects homes purchased after 14th December 2017.

Additionally, tax payers will no longer be able to deduct interest on home equity loans, unless the money has been used for renovations or other home improvements.

Furthermore, the overall deduction limit on any state and local tax (which is a combination of income tax, real estate tax or sales tax) will be capped at $10,000.

According to Forbes, "since most homes in this country are worth far less than $750,000, this change alone will not increase housing costs for the majority of home buyers".

You must check the current rules in the country you are planning to invest in before relying on any savings from this.

Additionally, some countries (such as NZ) allow rental property losses to be offset against income tax on other income. However, many countries (such as the UK) do not allow this. Therefore, be sure to check the taxation rules in your country to get clarity on this. **Always seek professional advice on tax related matters.**

TYPES OF PROPERTIES AND INVESTMENTS

The main focus of this book is on residential real estate. But for a comprehensive list, below are the key categories of real estate:

1. **Residential real estate** - houses, units, flats or apartments, townhouses and lifestyle blocks
2. **Commercial or industrial real estate** - Office space, retail space, warehouses, farmland, factories and mines.

The returns of the different categories can vary substantially. Investing in commercial real estate requires substantial knowledge and capital, however, it has many advantages:

1. Higher yields (returns).
2. Longer leases.
3. Costs are borne by the tenant (unlike in the case of residential property).

Below are some recommended books if you would like to learn more about commercial real estate:

1. **The Real Estate Game:** The Intelligent Guide to Decision Making and Investment by William J Poorvu
2. **Confessions of a Real Estate Entrepreneur:** What It Takes to Win in High-Stakes Commercial Real Estate by James A. Randel
3. **Commercial Real Estate Analysis and Investments** 3rd Edition by Geltner et al

FORMS OF TENURE OR TITLE

1. FREEHOLD (FEE SIMPLE) PROPERTY

Freehold property is where there is no time limit to the ownership of the land on which the property sits. In other words, the owner owns both the physical property and the land on which it sits in perpetuity.

According to Sullivan Property:

"A fee simple buyer is given title (ownership) of the property, which includes the land and any improvements to the land in perpetuity. Aside from a few exceptions, no one can legally take that real estate from an owner with fee simple title. The fee simple owner has the right to possess, use the land and dispose of the land as he wishes: sell it, give it away, trade it for other things, lease it to others, or pass it to others upon death."

In Australia this type of title is known as the **Torrens Title** and in the US and New Zealand it is known as **Fee Simple**.

Most residential property in New Zealand and Australia tends to be freehold. Most houses (rather than flats/apartments) in the UK also tend to be freehold.

The majority of real estate in the US is freehold; however, in certain states such as Hawaii, property is — in some cases — purchased on a leasehold basis.

2. LEASEHOLD PROPERTY

Leasehold property has a time limit to its ownership and there is a monthly or yearly amount to be paid for the rent of the land.

According to Sullivan Property:

"A leasehold interest is created when a fee simple land-owner (Lessor) enters into an agreement or contract called a ground lease with a person or entity (Lessee). A Lessee gives compensation to the Lessor for the rights of use and enjoyment of the land much as one buys fee simple rights; however, the leasehold interest differs from the fee simple interest in several important aspects. First, the buyer of leasehold real estate does not own the land; they only have a right to use the land for a pre-determined amount of time. Second, if leasehold real estate is transferred to a new owner, use of the land is limited to the remaining years covered by the original lease. At the end of the pre-determined period, the land reverts back to the Lessor, and is called reversion. Depending on the provisions of any surrender clause in the lease, the buildings and other improvements on the land may also revert to the lessor. Finally, the use, maintenance, and alteration of the leased premises are subject to any restrictions contained in the lease. During the lease term, typically there is a lease rent to be paid and there may be periodical increases throughout the term."

In Australia this type of property tends to be applicable for government properties in rural areas. In the UK many older flats are generally leasehold.

3. COMMONHOLD PROPERTY

Commonhold was a new type of property tenure that came about in the UK in 2002. It is similar to the US Condominium system. The land on which a building comprising of flats/apartments sits is registered as commonhold land, which means the land is jointly owned by the owners of the flats/apartments.

Commonhold is like freehold in that the owner of the property owns both the flat and its portion of the commonhold land in perpetuity.

In Australia this type of tenure is called **Group Title or Strata Title,** and in New Zealand this is known as a **Cross Lease.**

CAUTION

Before you buy any property ensure that you know whether it is freehold or leasehold and that the price you are paying reflects the nature of the property. Leasehold property tends to be cheaper than freehold, as you do not own the land and you have to pay *ground rent* (the rent you pay for the land the property sits on). The more expensive the ground rent is in each area or city, the bigger the difference is in price between leasehold and freehold properties in that location.

Additionally, the number of years left on a lease (i.e. the period that you have rights to the land your property sits on) is also very important and can have a major impact on the property value. In the UK, for example, new leases tend to be 99 years to 125 years. Once the lease period drops below 80 years, the property value can drop due to higher costs involved in extending the lease. The higher costs are due to something referred to as 'Marriage Value'.

Under the 1993 Leasehold Reform Act, the landlord is entitled to half of the increase in the value of the property when a less than 80-year lease is extended. This is called the Marriage Value or Marriage Fee because the value of the property plus longer lease (i.e. when married together) exceed the combined value of the separate entities. (Fletcher, n.d.)

Properties with short leases can also be harder to finance (Independent, 2012).

KEY RISKS OF BUYING PROPERTY

1. **Bubble bursts or short term drop in prices:** For example, New Zealand house prices (largely influenced by Auckland) have outpaced most other major countries. This is a major risk in any city (like Auckland) which has seen very high price increases over the last few years

   Mitigation:

   - Buy with a view to long term investing so that you can ride out any short-term price fluctuations.
   - Buy properties that are in upcoming areas and still offer good value for money. Also buy in cities that are growing but have a reasonable cost of living. If you follow these guidelines, if there is a price drop, any value reduction is likely to be far less than in the case of a high-value property.
   - Ensure that you can afford your mortgage payments so you can ride out any short-term dips in property values. Provided you can afford your mortgage payments, you should be in a good position in the long term.
   - Make sure you don't over-leverage yourself in case there is a price dip in the future. Banks may seek additional equity in case prices go down; however, if there is a nationwide drop in prices, the government would provide a certain level of protection as it would have to step in to ensure that a big portion of the population does not get thrown into financial distress.

2. **Stricter government regulation to curb price growth:** This would not affect any existing property you own but could affect future purchases.

   Mitigation:

- If you are a first-time buyer, the government will always try to safeguard that you are not disadvantaged. Investors are the main people affected in this situation.
- Advantages, such as offsetting tax using interest paid on mortgages, can be taken away. So, make sure you are not overly reliant on any such benefits. There was a time when depreciation costs for the overall property could be used to offset tax in New Zealand; for example, but this benefit was taken away some years back. (See footnote on changes per the ird.govt.nz website)[1]

3. **Increase in interest rates:** Whilst interest rate drops sometimes happen and can benefit you, they can also increase at any stage and put you in financial distress.

Mitigation:

- Always be certain that you are not overstretching yourself with mortgage payments. It is best to buy something less expensive than to overstretch (see section on What to Buy, Chapter 4, for further details)
- If you are caught out by increased interest rates and you cannot afford the payments, then you could either downsize or find ways to save in other areas.

---

[1] "Budget 2010 introduced changes to the depreciation rate of buildings. The changes were intended to make New Zealand's tax rules more neutral by recognising that allowing depreciation on long-lived buildings and the application of depreciation loading on certain assets provides tax depreciation rates in excess of true economic deprecation rates.

The depreciation rate of buildings with long-estimated useful lives has been changed to 0%. This new rate applies to all such buildings regardless of when they were purchased. This change is intended to make New Zealand's tax rules more neutral and non-distortionary." (New Zealand Inland Revenue)

- When interest rates are low, try to fix the term for as long as possible as this will ensure that you are not suddenly hit with major interest rate hikes and have time to plan for any future increases. You may sometimes feel that you've missed out on an interest rate decrease as your rate was fixed, but you can think of it like insurance; it may come at a cost, but it keeps you away from financial disasters.

4. **Major maintenance issues:** Maintenance will be required for your property at one stage or another and sometimes you can be hit with major and expensive repairs.

   Mitigation:

   - Make sure that you get the property fully checked by a professional before purchasing it to avoid being faced with any surprises (e.g. major leakage issues or foundation problems, etc.).
   - Also, always allow for some maintenance expenses in your budget. Regular proactive maintenance will make certain that you do not encounter big issues with big expenses at a later stage, e.g. regular service of your boiler will extend its lifespan. The same applies to the spouting and drainage systems.
   - If you do not have sufficient funds and are hit with a major repair you may be able to extend your mortgage or borrow through other means. If you do take this option, try to pay down the additional loan as quickly as you can so that you are not in excessive debt.

5. **Natural disasters or other damage (e.g. fire):** These are rare but can happen and catch you out.

   Mitigation:

- Know what types of disasters can occur in the area you are looking to buy and get insurance coverage for those and other general issues such as fire. In cases where there is no insurance coverage for certain natural disasters, there may be government support — seek advice from a professional on insurance matters.

6. **Tenancy issues (e.g. tenant not paying rent):** If you are renting your property there is a good chance that you will face some tenancy issue at one stage or another — particularly if you are renting to the lower socio-economic classes.

   Mitigation:

   - Use a reputable professional property manager to manage your property so they find good tenants for you and ensure that all procedures are followed.
   - If you do not use a property manager, be certain that you clearly understand and follow rules (e.g. how the bond should be lodged, how should notices be served, etc.).
   - Get rental protection insurance for any damage or rent not received - *This insurance has helped me on at least two occasions by recovering thousands of dollars that I could have lost where tenants either damaged the property and/or were in major rental arrears. I found that it was well worth paying the insurance premiums for this.*

7. **Rental property remaining vacant and impacting your rental returns:** If the rental market is down or if you don't advertise your property appropriately, you could end up with a higher than expected vacancy rate.

   Mitigation:

   - You must advertise and market your property accurately.

- Use property agents rather than trying to rent privately to save fees — as this can lose you more money than what you would pay in agent fees.
- Do not overprice your property. I have seen so many people leave a property vacant for 2 weeks or more just because they want to get $10 per week extra. 2 weeks of lost rent (say where weekly rental is $500) is worth $1,000. If you reduce your rent by $10 per week you would only lose $520 — so which option would you rather go with?

8. **Less liquid investment compared to shares or bonds:** It generally takes longer to sell a property than other investment classes such as shares and bonds. If you need money in an emergency and need to sell your asset, it would take longer to do so, as selling property can take a bit of time (weeks or even months sometimes).

Mitigation:

- You need to ensure that you have sufficient liquid assets to cover any emergencies or try to use the equity in your property to borrow more (while ensuring you are not over-gearing) if possible.

CHAPTER 2: PROPERTY VALUATION AND VALUE DRIVERS

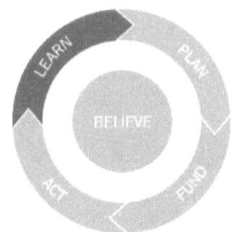

HOW IS PROPERTY VALUED?

I would encourage you to try to read this part as it will really help demystify the whole property valuation process. But if the formulas and math don't tickle your fancy, feel free to skim read it or skip over it.

There are three key types of valuation methods:

1. Using the yield approach
2. Comparison to recent sales of similar properties in the area
3. The Discounted Cash Flow method (DCF) — this is mainly used for the valuation of commercial property

Property valuers tend to use a combination of methods 1 and 2 to value residential property.

METHOD 1: USING THE YIELD APPROACH

The basic aspects of property valuation are so simple that you may find it hard to believe. If you can understand the formula below, then you can begin to estimate and get a real sense of property values.

There are three parts to the formula and if you have two of the three inputs, you can then swap the equation around as necessary to get the third part.

- Value (V) = property value
- Yield (Y) = the annual rental return of the property in percentage terms
- Annual Rent (R) = equals 12 times the monthly rent or 52 times the weekly rent (OK, maybe this didn't need an explanation!)

Below are the formulas:

- $V = R / Y$ OR
- $Y = R / V$ OR
- $R = Y / V$

It is also worth bearing in mind that at the end of the day the market value of anything is what a willing buyer is happy to pay a willing seller. This does play into the formula below through the Yield (Y) aspect of it.

Don't despair if you are confused at this stage or haven't yet understood the formulas. The examples below will simplify this for you swiftly.

Let's take a very simple example of how to apply these formulas:

1. Figuring out the value when you know the rent and average yields in the area:
   o Rent of house = $2,250 p.m. (i.e. annual rent = $27,000)
   o Yields in the area for a typical house = 3%
   o Therefore, Value of property = $27,000 / 3% = $900,0000

2. Figuring out the yield of a property when you know the rent and value of the property:

- Rent of house = $2,250 p.m. (i.e. annual rent = $27,000)
- Value of property = $900,0000
- Therefore Yields = $27,000/$900,000 = 3%

3. Figuring out the rent of a property when you know the yields and values of the properties in the area
   - Yields in the area for a typical house = 3%
   - Value of property = $900,0000
   - Rent of house = 3% x $900,000 = $27,000 ($2,250 p.m.)

METHOD 2: THE COMPARISON OF SIMILAR SALES METHOD

In this method the valuer will look at recent sales of similar properties in the area and on the street. This will give them a rough idea of the market value of the property and they can then make upward or downward adjustments depending on the specifics of the property being valued (e.g. is it in better or worse condition, is it larger or smaller, is it in a better part of the neighbourhood, etc.).

For example, imagine you want to buy a 4-bedroom house with 2 bathrooms on a plot of land that is 600 square meters (sqm) or 6,458 square feet in size.

The valuer would look at similar sales on the street and in the area. Let us imagine the valuer found the following recent sales:

- 3-bedroom house with 1 bathroom on 500sqm plot (similar area and condition): $700,000
- 4-bedroom house with 1 bathroom on 550sqm plot (slightly worse condition but similar area): $800,000
- 4-bedroom house with 2 bathrooms on 800sqm plot (but in a better part of the area and with much higher end finishing): $1,000,000

The above information would lead the valuer to conclude that the value of the house in question is somewhere between $800,000 and $1,000,000 and then he/she could refine as necessary and, in this example, perhaps conclude the value is $900,000 (combining the similar sales method with the valuation approach described in Method 1 above).

Another metric that is useful in establishing the value of the property by comparison is the price per square metre for the built-up part of the property. So let's say the average price of a flat in a given suburb is £5,000/sqm, then a 100 sqm property will be worth roughly around £500,000. However, this would then be adjusted for various factors such as total size of the land on which the property sits, the condition of the property, its exact location, etc.

METHOD 3: THE DISCOUNTED CASH FLOW OR DCF METHOD

Please feel free to skip this section as it is only meant for anyone who wants to have a deeper knowledge of the valuation of commercial real estate or more complex residential investments. However, I would encourage you to at least skim read this to get an idea of the process.

The DCF method is a technique to discount cash income and outgoings over a period of time back to the present value.

This sounds somewhat complicated but let us go through a simple example of what present value means. If someone gives you $1,000 today or $1,000 a year from now, is this the same value for you? Clearly not, as if you got the $1,000 today you could invest it (e.g. in a savings account) and get a return on this money. In other words, the $1,000 today is worth more than the $1,000 a year from now.

Imagine you have $1,000 and you can invest it in a bank and obtain interest of 5% on this investment. A year from now, you will therefore have $1,050 (ignoring any tax or fees for simplicity purposes). Now let us flip that around; if someone gave you $1,050 a year from now, what is its present value? The present value is $1,000 based on the same discount factor of 5%.

To value real estate using the DCF method you need the following details to work out your cash inflows and outflows:

1. Annual rent
2. Annual operating costs (Excluding interest costs and taxes)
3. Capital expenditure (CAPEX)
4. Annual depreciation and amortisation[2]
5. Tax rate

You also need the following information to compute the present value of your investment:

1. Expected annual growth rate of income and expenses (Growth)
2. Period of investment
3. Cost of capital (or Discount Factor)

According to investinganswers.com:

"Cost of capital refers to the opportunity cost of making a specific investment. It is the rate of return that could have been earned by putting the same money into a different investment with equal risk. Thus, the cost of capital is the rate of return required to persuade the investor to make a given investment."

---

[2] According to Investopedia, amortisation refers to the spreading out of capital expenses for intangible assets over a specific duration (usually over the asset's useful life) for accounting and tax purposes.

You then compute expected Earnings before Interest & Tax (EBIT) for each year.

EBIT = Rent (Revenue) – Operating Costs – Depreciation – Amortisation

(Note: the dashes above and in other formulas represent the minus sign)

You then compute the "free cash flow" ownership using the below formula:

Free Cash Flow = ((1 – Tax Rate) x EBIT) + Depreciation + Amortisation – CAPEX – Net Change in Working Capital

If the period of investment is in perpetuity (i.e. with no foreseen end date), the following formula is then used to compute the value expressed in terms of 'Net Present Value' (NPV):

NPV = FCF for First Year / (Cost of Capital – Growth)

However, if the investment has a pre-determined period and non-variable cash flows, the following "annuity" formula can be used:

NPV = FCF for First Year x $(1 - (1 + \text{Cost of Capital})^{-n})$ / Cost of Capital)

A simple model in Microsoft Excel can also be used to compute the value. This can even account for varying financial figures in different years (e.g. different rates of growth, interest, tax, etc.).

Let us take a very simple example. Imagine you have the opportunity to buy a building and your investment horizon is 5 years (i.e. you would sell it after 5 years). The building is being sold at $3.5m and you want to know if this is a good investment

- Annual rent = $500,000
- Annual expenses = 20% of rent
- CAPEX = $50,000 p.a.
- Depreciation = $50,000 p.a.
- Tax rate = 20%

- Cost of capital = 10% (this reflects the risk of investing in this type of building)
- Expected growth rate for rent and expenses = 2.5%
- Period of investment = 10 years
- Value of property at disposal = purchase price growing at 2.5% p.a.

	Today	Year 1	Year 2	Year 3	Year 4	Year 5
Purchase price & fees	-$3,500,000					
Annual rent = $500,000 growing at 2% p.a.		$500,000	$512,500	$525,313	$538,445	$551,906
Annual expenses = 20% of rent		-$100,000	-$102,500	-$105,063	-$107,689	-$110,381
CAPEX = $50,000 p.a. growing at 2% p.a.		-$50,000	-$51,250	-$51,250	-$51,250	-$51,250
Depreciation (Assume same as CAPEX)		-$50,000	-$51,250	-$51,250	-$51,250	-$51,250
EBIT (= Rent - Expense - Depreciation)		$350,000	$358,750	$369,000	$379,506	$390,275
Property Value at disposal growing at 2% p.a.						$4,480,296
Tax = 20% on income and capital gains		-$70,000	-$71,750	-$73,800	-$75,901.25	-$274,114
Free cashflow	-$3,500,000	$280,000	$287,000	$295,200	$303,605	$4,596,457
Net Present Value	$274,928					

Based on the above model, the NPV of the investment is almost $275k. Provided the NPV is over $0, it implies that it is a good investment. In other words, it is giving you a return over and above your "hurdle" rate (or the discount factor of 10% in this case).

Another way of working this model would be to *not* enter a purchase price and let the model give you an NPV based on that. However, as you would not know the value of the property at disposal, the simplified NPV perpetuity formula would be more appropriate where you assume that you would own the property in perpetuity.

Remember the NPV formula for cash flows in perpetuity = cash flow in first year / (cost of capital - growth)

The below table computes the cash flows for the first year:

	Year 1
Purchase price & fees	
Annual rent = $500,000 growing at 2% p.a.	$500,000
Annual expenses = 20% of rent	-$100,000
CAPEX = $50,000 p.a. growing at 2% p.a.	-$50,000
Depreciation = Same as CAPEX	-$50,000
EBIT (= Rent - Expense - Depreciation)	$350,000
Value of property at disposal growing at 2% p.a.	
Tax = 20% on income and capital gains	$70,000
Free cashflow	$280,000

Therefore, NPV based on the perpetuity formula = $280,000 / (10% - 2.5%) = $3,733,333. To this end, you could pay a max price of $3,733,333 to make an economic profit with this investment (i.e. ensure that your return at least equals your cost of capital).

DRIVERS OF PROPERTY VALUE GROWTH

Below are some key factors that affect the growth of property values

1. Purchasing power growth

Purchasing power growth results in more people being able to afford homes, hence there is increased demand. If supply does not keep up with the population growth, then economics dictates that prices should rise. As you can see in the charts below, using Australia as an example, there is a strong correlation between property price growth and increase in GDP or purchasing power. However, in recent years, house price growth has outpaced GDP growth, which has caused the fear of a bubble in many markets.

Figure 6: HOUSE PRICE VS. GDP GROWTH IN AUSTRALIA - 1961 TO 2011
(Reserve Bank of Australia, 2011)

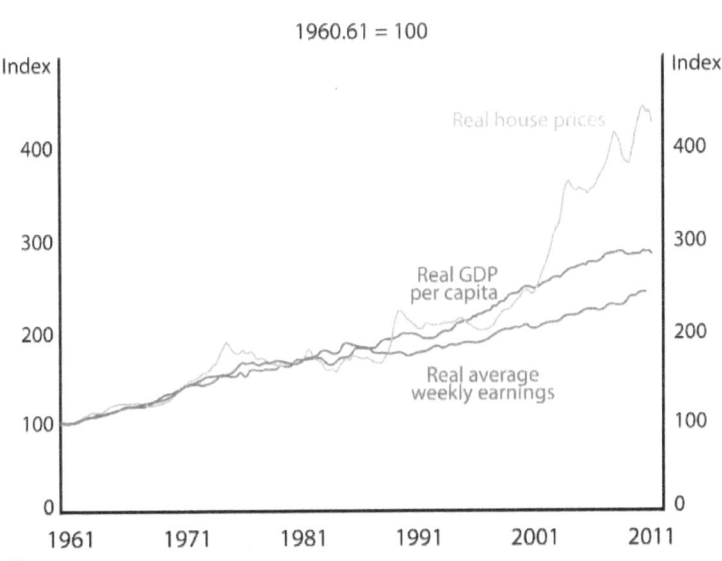

Sources: Abelson and chung (2005), ABS, Australian Treasury, FEIA

2. Population growth e.g. due to immigration or increased urbanisation

Immigration increases demand for housing and if supply does not keep up with the population growth, then economics dictates that prices should rise. As you can see from the chart below showing net migration versus annual house price changes in New Zealand, there is a strong correlation between the property value increases and net immigration.

Figure 7: MIGRATION VERSUS HOUSE PRICES IN NEW ZEALAND (Global Property Guide, 2016)

Net Migration 000's (left scale)   Annual house price change (right scale)
Source: Real Estate Institute of New Zealand & SNZ

3. Insufficient supply to keep up with growing demand

If housing demand growth outstrips supply growth, as in the case of Auckland and Sydney in recent years, then basic economics dictates that prices will increase. And we have seen this happen year after year in these cities and similar cities in the last decade or so.

4. Investor Speculation

Property value growth can sometimes be driven entirely due to speculation as more and more investors buy property with the expectation of value increase. Speculation without fundamental factors driving growth is *very dangerous* as it can cause an artificial bubble, which will have to burst at one stage or another. There are fears that there are artificial bubbles in a few cities around the world such as London, Sydney, Auckland and Vancouver. It is for this reason that you must really ensure that you are investing in property for the long term rather than trying to make a quick buck in the short term. You also need to ensure that you do your homework and choose your investments wisely (i.e. where growth is being driven by solid fundamentals and there is good potential for long-term growth even if there could be some dips in the short term).

SECTION B - HOW TO GET STARTED

"Start where you are. Use what you have. Do what you can."

-Arthur Ashe

CHAPTER 3: THE FIRST STEPS AND SETTING OBJECTIVES

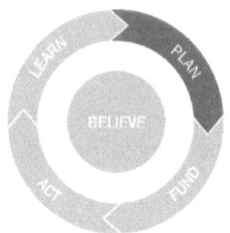

THE PHILOSOPHY OF BUYING PROPERTY

Let us first start by thinking about the philosophy of buying a property.

I refer to buying property and investing in property interchangeably, as I see the purchase of property as an investment whether it is for personal use or to rent out. Purchasing a home requires substantial money up front and then large monthly mortgage payments. Rather than thinking of your home as an expense, if you see it as an investment then this thought process leaves you in a much healthier financial situation as you will:

- Keep emotion out of your purchasing decisions and this in turn will stop you from overpaying for a property.
- Make a sound financial assessment before buying the property. For example:
    a. Will this be a good long-term investment?
    b. Will you acquire quality tenants and get good rental returns if you must rent the property out for whatever reason (e.g. if you move out of town or overseas for a while)?

    c. Will you be able to sell the property reasonably fast and get a good resale value if you need to sell it?

- Avoid over capitalising the property
- Time the purchase well

Someone may argue that: *"When I buy my home I do not want to compromise on my personal space and quality of life"*. Just because you consider the above points and buy in a financially astute matter, it does not mean that you cannot also get something you will be very happy to stay in. At least you will have considered the financial aspects and found a suitable compromise.

When my wife and I moved to London we rented a flat for the first 3 years or so. Once I had found a decent job after completing my MBA, and we felt that London was going to be our home for a while, we decided to buy our own property. However, rather than thinking purely from an emotional standpoint regarding the purchase, we decided to buy the property as a long-term investment so that it would be a sensible purchase even if we left London. Therefore, we bought a lovely flat in St Johns Wood, very close to the Lords Cricket Ground. It was a ground floor flat with a fine garden. As fate would have it, after two years we got the opportunity to move overseas with my company. As we had made a sensible purchase, we found good tenants quickly and were able to comfortably cover our mortgage payments from that rental income.

BELIEVING AND THE BROADER MINDSET

Before you even get started, the most important aspect of the entire process is that you believe that you can achieve your objectives. I am a strong believer that, 'if you do not believe then you shall not get what you want'. I have dedicated an entire chapter to this and other deeper aspects linked to this subject. See **Chapter 15** for further details on this.

KEY STEPS TO GETTING STARTED

OK, so this is a bit of a cliché, but how do you eat an elephant? Well, one bite at a time! How did they build the wall of China? One brick at a time! How do you write a book? One word at a time! I think you get the message!

If you find it challenging to begin your property quest, the key to purchasing a property (or to expanding your property investments) is to break down the challenge and to take one baby step at a time.

Now I know we all feel that such words are easy to say but it is much harder to do the actual work. I can assure you that our tasks and goals are often a lot easier to accomplish than what we think they are when we are initially faced with them.

Let me take some time to explain, as I believe this is one of the most critical points of the book. What often stops us from doing something or from taking action is procrastination. Let us take the simple example of breaking down a wall. When you look at this big wall, you see this massive task, and with all the right intentions you think that you will find the time to do it properly — maybe even later today or tomorrow. And somehow the later today or tomorrow never comes, or it takes a very long time to arrive!

I am also guilty of being a procrastinator at times and this is how I try to get around such a mindset — I start a very big task by taking the first tiny step and then, often leaving it. Let us go back to the example of the wall. If I want to break down a wall, I simply spend a few minutes to remove one single brick. You may ask what the big deal is about that. Well, accomplishing such a task really is a big deal — the next time I look at that wall, I will no longer see it as a humongous wall. I see that one brick has already been removed, which makes it very easy for me to remove the next brick, then the next one, and the next one, and before I know it, the whole wall is down!

If I am putting together a PowerPoint presentation, the first thing I do is find the right template and put together a simple framework. It then becomes an easy task to fill in the blanks. If I find a particular slide hard to complete in a given moment, I skip to a slide I'm sure I can complete at that time and I can always revisit the harder one a bit later. Rather than thinking of the presentation as one BIG task, I break it down and attack it bit by bit, and I complete the work in no time! – This is what I was taught as best practice and it really works for me. I am passing on my learnings and I hope that you will find your own ways to achieve this if you are also the victim of procrastination.

I really urge you to try this. Take that first step and the rest will somehow follow! If you want to write a book, open a new Microsoft Word document and simply write the title. If you want to buy a property, start by writing down what sort of property you want to buy or by simply opening a real estate website and filtering the type of property you want to buy. If you want to cook dinner, just put a few ingredients on your kitchen bench. If you want to go to the gym and are feeling lazy, put your gym gear on the bed or wear it — you will be amazed at how you will suddenly think about actually taking the next step. You might even end up doing a few press-ups or sit-ups at home, which is far better than doing nothing.

I am also a big believer in solving a problem using the 'top down' approach. First, you must have a big picture in mind to break down into key chunks and then continuously break down each chunk into further chunks. Let us take the example of this book. I literally started by writing the title of the book and then thought of the key chapters I would like in it. I then took each chapter and broke it down into sub headings and so forth.

You can also think of it like a holiday — you first need to know where you would like to go. You then break the task down into sub tasks: Where do I want to go? How will I get there? What do I need to take? Another way of thinking about this is how a building is constructed. You start with an idea of what you want to build, where you want to build it and roughly what you want to spend. Then the architect comes up with a concept design, which then evolves into the deeper layers of detail. The foundation is then built, the structure comes next and finally we have the finishing.

I am not saying that there is a single correct way of doing things, but I find that working from the bottom up takes a lot longer and often leaves you lost, e.g. figuring out how many windows a given room will have when you do not even know the size of the building or where it will be located. This may sound like a silly example, but how many times have you seen people stuck in irrelevant detail when the main issues are still left hanging.

There is a good book by Barbara Minto, *The Pyramid Principle*, which explains this top down approach really well from the perspective of preparing documents or presentations. The same principles apply to any complex activity.

In my experience, the key questions to ask when putting together your road map for getting on the property ladder are as follows:

1. What is your objective and what is your investment horizon?
2. What, where and when to buy?
3. How to find the right property?
4. How to raise money to buy?
5. How to measure the financial return of your investment?

6. How to execute the property purchase?

WHAT IS YOUR OBJECTIVE AND WHAT IS YOUR INVESTMENT HORIZON?

To achieve goals, one must have clear objectives. And to have clear objectives, you need to know exactly what you want. Do you want a single property? Do you want 10 properties? Do you want to make $50m wealth from those properties? What do you want?

In terms of a given specific purchase, what are your objectives? Are they simply about getting on the property ladder? Is it to purchase a long-term home? Is it to buy and let as an investment? Is it to buy, improve and sell, or to keep? Is it to upgrade? And what are your longer-term plans?

Additionally, you need to be very clear on the investment period. Whilst in the long term, real estate investment is very likely going to give positive returns, in the short-term, values can be very volatile — you could lose money, particularly if you are not a seasoned investor. Personally, when I invest in real estate I look at a minimum 10-year horizon for the investment. Additionally, my philosophy is to buy and hold. There are substantial transaction costs when you buy a property, and if you make the right purchase the only reason to sell is if you want to release capital to make a bigger, more attractive investment, or if you are retired and want to free up the cash for living purposes.

In fact, going beyond purchasing or investing in property, I am a strong believer of having clear goals in life. My recommendation would be to set goals as below:

1. **1-year goals:** These should be very realistic and just require a slight stretch to achieve (e.g. I want to save $10,000 this

year; I want to get a promotion; I want to pay off $5,000 of debt, etc.)

2. **3-year goals:** These should still have a certain sense of reality but should have a substantial stretch to where you are (e.g. I want to buy a large, 3-bed home in a specific city or suburb; I want to increase my salary by 50%; I want to get a managerial role; I want an executive role, etc.)

3. **5-10-year goals:** These should be aspirational and in the 'dreamland' category (e.g. I want to own 10 houses; I want to make $1,000,000; I want to own my own company with a staff of over 1,000, etc.)

I once read somewhere that most people overestimate what they can do in 1 year and totally underestimate what they can achieve in 10. What did you achieve in the last year? What did you think you would achieve? Now compare that to the last 5-10 years! I bet you that you will notice a massive difference in what you thought you would achieve and what you actually achieved in these two different scenarios.

If you are really keen to invest in property then clearly this objective has to be a key part of your short, mid and long-term goals as appropriate.

WHY HAVE MORE THAN ONE PROPERTY?

If possible, you should always strive to own at least 2 properties to fully benefit from the appreciation of property values. If you only own a single home, then even if property values appreciate, you will not be able to make use of those funds unless you sell your house and downsize or rent. You could also get some benefit if you use the added value/equity to take on a higher mortgage — but then you will have to pay more interest.

If you have 2 properties, then when you retire you could sell the second home and keep your primary home, thus providing money for your retirement. Alternatively, you could live off the rent of the second home rather than sell it. Having a second home gives you a much better chance to live in your primary home without having to downsize.

HOW I STARTED

It was the early 2000s and my girlfriend had moved from Paris to come and live with me in New Zealand some months earlier.

I was in my late 20s. I working as an IT consultant and doing very well. I had a very good salary and I was one of the top talents in the company. I was even driving a flash BMW 5 series. One would expect that I would have been in a great financial situation. On the contrary, I had zero savings. In fact, I was in debt. My girlfriend could not believe it when I told her that we did not have enough money to go for a holiday to Bali (a non-expensive holiday location). I eventually used my credit card to pay for my share of the holiday and maxed it out! Does that ring a bell on something similar you have done?

I grew up in an upper middle-class family. My father had a thriving business, selling coffins and providing other burial services. I was fortunate enough to manage this business for a few months before starting my university. My father was an incredible personality — larger than life! He grew up in a family that had been wealthy but had lost everything by the time he was born. Growing up in poverty, sometimes struggling to make enough money for food during the day, he always dreamt of making it big. And he did. However, because of the stigma of having been poor, he wanted to show his wealth, and more than that, he wanted to help others — pretty much anyone he met. I had 4 siblings, but we always had a few other people (random ones, sometimes) living in our house. On average we were about 12 people living in our house, but if on any given day we had guests (which was pretty much every day) there would always be enough food to feed everyone — even if a family of 10 visited us! I still wonder how we made this happen! That is why I probably consider my mum as super woman! The unfortunate thing is that we sometimes lived beyond our means and because of this, we were at times in debt.

I have described all the above to give context to my mindset. Whilst I always had the intention of living within my means, I still ended up with some debts for my tertiary studies (not a bad thing) and for other things, such as my car and furniture.

Everything changed for me because one day a good friend from university invited me to join this exciting new venture. It was Omega — a direct marketing organisation. Whilst I eventually decided that this type of programme was not my calling, what it did do for me was open my eyes. I met many people who wanted to succeed, and who gave me access to a wealth of knowledge through books and speakers, and I got to see how some of my friends succeeded in investing in property.

Being very ambitious, eventually, my girlfriend (Audrey) and I decided to start up a small business. Audrey's mother was happy to lend us $7,000 for it. Audrey came up with the idea of having a boutique store to sell French lingerie. We even went as far as identifying potential stores to rent and writing a full-fledged business plan — fairly amateurish when I think about what we wrote at that time!

Then one day, while we were having a small picnic in Mission Bay (a lovely seaside suburb of Auckland), an idea came to mind. Having seen how my friends had been doing well at investing in real estate, (with one of them having built a portfolio of more than

5 properties in about 2 years), I suggested to Audrey that we use the money in a more risk averse way and invest in property.

Audrey liked my idea, but we did not immediately make a choice. We kept on umming and ahhing and I even went to a seminar where some new apartment developments were being advertised, and I had a chat with the developer. Still unable to make up our minds, one day we decided to let fate choose for us. We decided to wait for some sort of sign. To our surprise, we saw that same developer I had met some days back when we went out for dinner at the Sky City's revolving restaurant in the heart of Auckland City. Audrey and I both laughed about it and agreed that this was our sign and we even told the developer about it!

We paid a small deposit to the developer and I also spoke to my bank and they informed me that they would be willing to lend me 95% of the value of the property and would lend a maximum of $125,000.

Some days later, I heard bad rumours about the development we were getting into. The building was supposed to go up on an established area of Queen Street in central Auckland, yet there was not the slightest sign of anything even remotely being planned or built. I had very little savings and I did not want to waste what I did have saved on a bad purchase. As I was very close to my boss at the time, I asked him for some advice. He told me that it would be better to invest in a unit or house rather than a new build apartment (this was relevant given my situation and the nature of the apartment market at that time). I discussed this with Audrey, and we decided to pull out of the deal. We were fortunate enough that we hadn't yet paid the full deposit and we also received our partial deposit of $1,000 back! (This may not sound like a large sum of money, but it was a big amount to me at that time). I later found out that some of the investors who had put in much larger deposits did not get their money back, as the *developer went under. The development has not happened do date — so we made a lucky escape!*

We then started looking for an investment unit or small house. I quickly realised that Audrey had a knack for finding good investment properties — she found us a property going for $125,000 but had a market value of over $140,000. However, because it was a contract that was being on-sold, we needed to pay an additional $7,000 to get ownership of the contract. We therefore needed to raise another $7,000 or so.

I decided to sell my car to raise the shortfall in funds. Amazingly, I managed to sell my car for $10,000 (an amount much higher than I thought I would get given the age and condition of the car), as a nice Englishman fell in love with it. This not only filled that cash gap but also contributed $3,000 towards my purchase of a smaller, cheaper car.

We bought the property and saved as much as we could in the next couple of months to raise money to make improvements to it. Up to that point, I had never done any handy work and barely had any experience with it. However, my wife and I rolled up our sleeves and went to work and spent evenings and weekends improving it. I still cannot believe how we managed to make the improvements with the tiny amount of cash we had raised. But somehow, we did, and we managed to get tenants very quickly. And that was the start of our property adventure!

Our mindset to money and investments completely changed after that and I am very thankful to say that I have never ever taken any 'bad debt' after that.

A key point I would like to highlight here is the concept of 'Synchronicity'.

Synchronicity is a word coined by the Swiss psychologist Carl Jung to describe the temporally coincident occurrences of acausal events, i.e. a pattern of connection that is not explained by causality. Below are examples of synchronicity (www.crystalinks.com, 2017):

- *"You are suffering with financial difficulties, yet money for basic expenses such as rent, food, and utilities, always manifests.*
- *You have just received your last cheque from unemployment when suddenly a job comes along.*
- *You drive to a place where parking is "next to impossible" and someone pulls out of a parking spot or it is waiting for you.*
- *You meet someone who interests you and touches your soul. Through synchronicity that person seems to come into your life over and over again. You begin to feel a destiny with that person. You begin to think with your heart instead of your head. You connect with that person. In some cases, the karma between the two people is positive but in many cases, you have attracted that person into your life for a learning lesson whether you are aware of it or not."*

Once I started to mingle with the right people (i.e. those who were successful investors and property buyers) and I started reading books, my mindset changed. My wife and I suddenly saw the potential to be entrepreneurs. Although we initially thought that we could not afford to start a business or buy a property, after changing our mindset, suddenly avenues opened up. We realised we could borrow some money and sell my car to raise enough cash to buy a small property. The same property we bought for $125,000 is now worth multiples of this figure. We recently added a third bedroom to it, which has also helped with the value gain.

We also left it to the "universe" to decide whether we went ahead with the business or purchased a property. The universe definitely made the right decision for us. You can replace the word "universe" here with "God" or any other form of spiritual belief. Whilst the initial apartment purchase did not work out, we still ended up buying a property and a much better one! I am certain that if I had not changed my mindset, I would still be in debt today regardless of the income I would be making!

CHAPER 4: WHAT, WHERE AND WHEN TO BUY

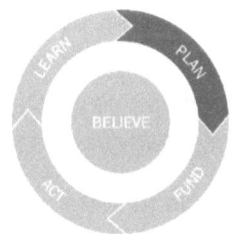

BUY WHAT YOU CAN AFFORD AND BUY IT NOW

Quoting home prices using averages can sometimes be misleading. Yes, the cost of an average home in London is close to £600,000, in Sydney it is over AU$1.1m and in Auckland it is well over NZ$800,000; however, if you are in your mid-twenties, are you necessarily looking for an average home?

When I bought my first investment, it cost me $125,000. However, the average home at that time cost probably around $300,000. Could I afford to buy an average home at that time? No. So rather than waiting I bought what I could afford, and it was the best decision I could have possibly made.

The question to ask yourself is: do you want an average home or some other fancy place, or do you want to get on the property ladder and do what it takes to get there?

Per the earlier chart on property prices, on average, property prices will always rise in the long term so getting on the property ladder, even if it means compromising on the type of property or location, is key.

Clearly, different people have different needs and will be in different financial positions. Therefore, rather than thinking of the average home or the home that your parents have or the home that your mates have, think about what your short and long-term goals are. If you can start with a 1-bed unit or apartment, then why not go for it and upsize later? At least if the prices continue to rise your 1-bed unit or apartment will have also appreciated in value and given you equity that you would otherwise not have. If the prices remain flat, then you could continue saving more and then upgrade when you are ready to do so.

Let us go through an example to better explain the point:

Say Nancy has savings of $100,000 and has been wanting to buy a 3-bed home worth $600,000. The bank informs her that they can only lend her a maximum of $480,000 (based on 80% lending). So Nancy decides that she will save $20,000 for another year. She manages to do extremely well and save that amount in one year; however, she finds that property prices have increased by 10% and now the same property is worth $660,000 so once again she finds herself short of money and even if she manages to quickly raise the shortfall, she ends up $60,000 worse off due to the increased cost of property. Looking at her total equity, it would be $120,000.

On the other hand, Nancy could have compromised and purchased a cheaper property (e.g. a smaller one, one in a different suburb, a townhouse rather than house, etc.) worth $500,000 and in one year's time her equity would be worth $150,000 (given the 10% growth in property values) plus her added savings of $20,000 her total equity would be $170,000.

So, Nancy would have been $50,000 better off by buying the property up front rather than waiting for a year.

One thing to note is that different types of property and different locations may have different growth rates; however, based on my philosophy of keeping it simple, get on the property ladder as soon as you can and keep growing your portfolio as fast as you can (while managing risk).

The above said, if you are already on the ladder and you are considering how you can best diversify and grow your portfolio in the long term, then it makes a lot of sense to think about your overall investment strategy and what type of property and location best serve your needs and then time your purchases accordingly.

AIM FOR A POSITIVE CASH FLOW PROPERTY

Aiming for a positive cash flow property is a key requisite for astute investors. In other words, the objective is to ensure that at least the interest payments and other property expenses (barring asset improvements and capital repayments) can be covered by the rental income. In order to determine that, you need to run numbers on your property as per the example below:

Purchase Price	400,000	
Fees & Stamp Duty (if any)	8,000	
Total Purchase Price	**408,000**	
Debt	240,000	= Current Mortgage Balance (assume 60%)
Rent (per month)	1,600	
Est. Vacancy Rate	3%	
Total Income (per annum)	**18,624**	= Monthly Rent x 12 x (1 - Vacancy Rate)
PM Fees (per annum)	1,920	= Approx 10% of Annual Rent
Insurance / Rates (per annum)	800	= Approx 0.2% of Purchase Price (as example)
Maintenance (per annum)	1,200	= Approx 0.3% of Purchase Price (as example)
Interest Rate	4.0%	
Interest Amount (per annum)	9,600	= Interest Rate x Current Mortgage Balance
Net Income	5,104	= Total Income - All Expenses
Tax (assuming 30% marginal rate)	1,531	
Net Income after Tax	3,573	
Gross Yield on Purchase Price	4.7%	
Net Yield on Purchase Price	1.3%	
Market Yield	4%	
Est. Property Value	480,000	= Annual Rent / Market Yield
Net Equity	240,000	= Property Value - Debt

If your property purchase is not paying for itself through rental income, then you will need to pay the shortfall with your own income — in essence, you are relying on potential capital gains in the future to make you money rather than relying on the property income to grow your wealth. If property values do not increase in the short to medium-term, then your finances could be constrained and rather than making money, you may end up losing it! Hence, regardless of the market, aim to have positive cash flow.

If you finance either all or a very large portion of a new property by leveraging equity in your existing property portfolio, then you should look at your overall portfolio returns rather than just the new property returns in isolation. I have been able to buy new properties a few times by purely using equity in my existing portfolio and either not putting in any equity or putting in a very small amount. In these cases, I have assessed returns on an overall portfolio basis, as looking at the new purchase in isolation would have been misleading.

BUY A PROPERTY THAT HAS POTENTIAL TO ADD VALUE

The ideal property to buy with an investor's hat is one which has potential for future value addition so that you can grow your wealth by adding value to the property at an appropriate time (e.g. when you have the time to focus on it and have the necessary funds). Examples of potential value adding properties are listed below. You will also find further details in Chapter 10, which is dedicated to adding value to your property.

1. **Run-down property in a good area:** You must have heard of the good old saying that it is better to buy the worst property on the best street rather than the best property on the worst street. Hence, if you can find a property that is run down and is in a good or excellent area, you could add substantial value to it by doing it up. And when it comes to doing up properties there does not have to be any hurry. You can take your time and do it up as you get the necessary funds. Clearly, if you can do it all at once, that is even better.

2. **Property with additional land that can be subdivided and developed:** If you can buy a property with sufficient land to subdivide, then you can almost guarantee decent returns once you can subdivide and develop the land. *I recently did that with one of my properties and whilst it is a lengthy process and takes serious effort and money, overall it gives decent returns.*

3. **Property that can be extended or improved** by adding other bedrooms, bathrooms, etc. or making a few changes; e.g. breaking down unnecessary walls to create more space, etc. Making these few extensions or improvements can result in a very good return on your investment and substantial value addition to your property. E.g. by adding a 3rd ensuite bedroom to one of my properties, I estimate that the value increased by up to $100,000.

4. **Property that can be re-developed**, e.g. where the property is in a high-density housing zone but has a single dwelling, which could be demolished and replaced by more dense dwellings. Redeveloping is capital intensive but if done properly, you could get a very healthy return on your investment. A good example of this is the street where I grew up in Nairobi. It was in the suburb of South B and when we lived there, the whole street only had large bungalows with at least 4 bedrooms. Now there are only multi-storey apartments on that entire street and in most of the surrounding areas.

5. **A growing/upcoming area where value addition will happen automatically:** If you buy in an upcoming area, or where there are going to be infrastructure improvements, the value of your property could increase at a much higher rate than other parts of the city. All this requires is a bit of research on any major infrastructure projects, e.g. new train stations, highways, etc. JLL gives an example of a suburb in Delhi, India, where prices almost doubled over a 4-year period due to the Delhi Metro, compared to other areas which experienced half that growth in the same period (JLL, 2014).

MAKE A SENSIBLE PROPERTY PURCHASE RATHER THAN FEAR A PROPERTY BUBBLE

Now some people may ask, "but what if there is a property bubble and what if the prices go down once I have bought my property?"

If anyone could predict market cycles and asset bubbles, then they should be billionaires — not just millionaires. No one knows where the economy will go or where any bubbles will burst (if indeed there *are* any bubbles).

Rather than fearing bubbles or economic downturns, you should think about what your investment plan is, and if you find a property that fits that plan, buy it! Make sure that you have sufficient equity and are comfortably able to afford the mortgage even if there is a slight increase in interest rates.

Regardless of what the property is worth on paper (and even if the value has dropped in the short term), if you are able to pay your mortgage and are able to ride out the slump, then you have little to worry about. In the long term, the likelihood is that the values will rise again. You, however, need to be more cautious if you are close to retirement and are planning to use the home equity to fund that retirement — if there is a perceived property bubble in your city then it might be better to invest in a safer class (such as bonds), or to invest in another location to avoid unnecessary risk.

If property prices drop, then your loan to value ratio will go up; however, the same would apply to everyone who owns a property and has a loan. Anything is possible, but it is very unlikely that banks will ask every single home owner to inject further equity, as this would cause a big chunk of the country's population to either lose their homes or go bankrupt. This would further reduce the property values (as supply would outstrip demand) and even more people would face financial distress. Governments tend to avoid such situations as it can result in a vicious cycle and utter chaos in the economy.

MY OWN APPROACH TO WHAT, WHERE AND WHEN TO BUY?

My personal philosophy is to focus on positive cash flow investments serving the middle-class market. My initial properties were more in the working-class category, but as I was able to gain more equity and raise more capital, I started investing in the middle-class segment of the market. I have more recently started focusing on developments and have even purchased an empty plot of land to develop either luxury holiday homes or apartments.

When I bought my first property, it was simply about getting on the property ladder. I had read numerous self-help books and talked to many inspiring people and all I wanted was to get at least one property. When I sold the idea of buying the property to my wife, we started researching all over Auckland, and through my wife's magic, we found a 2-bed unit but with a garage converted to a 3rd room in a decent area (Mt Wellington). An added benefit was that there was a new mall coming up a couple of kilometres away. Given the excellent price, the rental potential and the potential for value growth, it was a no brainer for us.

We could have waited to save more and bought a nicer property, but it was the best step we'd ever taken. In fact, the reason the owners were struggling to sell the property was that the neighbour had a mental disorder and was a hoarder. His entire property was like a war zone and his garden had a 3-foot layer of garbage throughout! This is not an exaggeration at all! As part of the tidy up of our property, we managed to convince him to allow us to clean up his garden. It took us two full weekends and two large skips with help from two friends to clear! As a gesture of gratitude, he offered me a cup of tea in a probably 100-year old, dented aluminium cup and I have to say that I rather enjoyed it!

I am not too fussed about the type of property, as I have a mixture of houses, units, flats and land. When I make a property purchase decision, below are the key things I focus on:

- *How much can I afford to buy the next property, and will I be able to raise enough finance?*
  - *Does the location of purchase allow me to get finance?*
  - *Do I need to get finance from a bank?*
  - *Can I co-invest with someone else?*
- *How do I want to expand my portfolio, i.e.?*
  - *Is it to get rental income?*
  - *Is it to focus on a capital growth area?*
  - *Is it to develop, etc.?*
- *Based on my portfolio expansion strategy, which country / city do I want to buy it in*
  - *I never purchase a property in a city that I do not intimately know. This is because it is critical for me to be able to understand the full market dynamics and have a clear idea of different locations. I also only focus on specific locations rather than buying in any willy-nilly area.*
- *Which type, and size of property can I buy, given my budget and desired location (e.g. house vs. unit and number of bedrooms)?*

Once I have answers to the above, my wife and I spend weeks searching for properties and we have often done this remotely using the internet. We often also end up finding private sellers and this is a bonus, as it saves agent fees for the buyer which enables us to get a better deal.

CHAPTER 5: HOW TO DETERMINE YOUR BUDGET AND FIND THE RIGHT PROPERTY

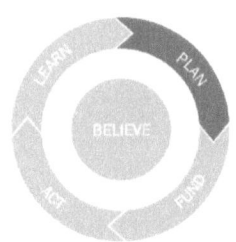

FIGURING OUT YOUR BUDGET

It is very important that you buy within your affordability and do not overextend yourself and end up in financial trouble. You, therefore, must ensure that you can afford both the initial property purchase costs and the ongoing monthly costs after the purchase.

Below are the key costs for the initial purchase and for the ongoing expenses. Make sure that you take these into consideration before you make a property purchase.

INITIAL PROPERTY PURCHASE:

- Property purchase price (this is the largest cost and the rest are very small costs compared to the actual property purchase)
- Stamp duty in certain countries such as the UK and Australia
- Other property-related costs
  - Valuation fees
  - Builder's report fees

- o   Share of rates
- Legal and associated expenses
  - o   Lawyer's fee
  - o   Title search and other similar fees
  - o   Transfer and mortgage registration fees
- Mortgage set up expenses
  - o   Loan application fees
  - o   Break fee for any existing loans (e.g. if upgrading home or changing lender)
- Other expenses
  - o   Relocation costs

ONGOING MONTHLY EXPENSES

- Monthly mortgage
- Property and contents insurance
- Council rates
- Utilities (water bills and electricity)
- Maintenance and repairs
- Property manager's fees (if renting out and using a property manager)

Let us take a practical example of looking at the affordability of buying a home and how you can plan that. You will recall from earlier in the book that a mortgage is considered affordable if it does not take up more than 40% of your net income. So, let us look at a hypothetical situation.

- Net family income: $85,000 per year or $7,083 per month - roughly the average take-home income of first-time home buying couples in New Zealand
- You already have savings of $50,000

- Your monthly savings are about $1,500 (yearly savings = $18,000)
- You need to have a 10% deposit as you qualify for this as a first home buyer
- You will incur the following transaction costs when buying a house:
  - Legal fees: $1,500
  - Valuation fees: $600
  - Other general costs: $200
  - Moving costs: $200
  - Total transaction costs = $2,500
- You are keen to save for another year and have total savings of $68,000
- After deducting the transaction costs, you are left with a deposit of about $65,000
- Hence, if you require a 10% deposit for your purchase, this implies that you can buy a property worth $650,000
- Now, let us also compute the mortgage payments so that you know that you will comfortably be able to pay them:
  - Loan amount = $585,000
  - Fixed interest rate for 3 years = 5%
  - Loan term = 30 years
  - Monthly mortgage = $3,140
- Let us check if this mortgage payment is affordable
  - $3,140 / $7,083 = 44.3%
- So, the above tells us that you would be too stretched and have an unaffordable mortgage if you purchase a property of $650,000 with a 10% deposit based on present interest rates
- You then decide to stick to a $600,000 property
- You still put in a deposit of $65,000 (a little over 10%)
- Your mortgage is therefore $535,000. The figures in this case would be as follows:
  - Loan amount = $535,000

- o Fixed interest rate for 3 years = 5%
- o Loan term = 30 years
- o Monthly mortgage = $2,899
- o Mortgage payment affordability = $2,899 / $7,083 = 40.5%
- Therefore, it is a financially astute decision to buy a slightly cheaper property at $600,000 (or ideally even lower) and to keep your mortgage affordable.

HOW TO FIND THE RIGHT PROPERTY

The most important thing is to make the right purchase, whether it is for a home you are going to live in (short or long term) or it is for investment purposes.

We have all heard the adage "location, location, location!" However, you can wish all you want to have a certain location and you may end up wasting a lot of time trying to buy in your dream location. My view is, buy reasonably quickly and make compromises as necessary, provided you are being sensible and thinking of the long-term picture. Cleary, if you can immediately buy in the ideal location, then go for it!

The starting point is to know how much you can afford to pay for the property (including all other expenses involved) and pay for the monthly mortgage, as well as other expenses. The next chapter gives detailed information about managing your finances and raising money for a property purchase. This should help you figure out when you can purchase and how much you will be able to afford.

A good way to find out how much you can afford is by checking any online mortgage affordability calculator, e.g.:

1. https://www.zillow.com/mortgage-calculator/house-affordability/ for the US,
2. https://www.hsbc.co.uk/1/2/mortgages/how-much-can-i-borrow?cid=HBEU:JDC:P1:MG:01:1709:056:Generic_Exact for the UK,
3. https://www.asb.co.nz/home-loans-mortgages/calculator-borrowing.html for NZ, and
4. https://www.yourmortgage.com.au/calculators/how-much-can-i-borrow/ for Australia

This should give you a fairly good idea of your property budget.

Once you know how much you can afford, a good next step would be to go to a website — like Zillow.com in the US, Zoopla.co.uk in the UK, Domain.com.au in Australia and Trademe.com in New Zealand — and search for properties, with a filter applied on the price of the property based on your budget. Repeat the process on as many property websites as possible. This should give you a reasonable idea of the types of properties you can get within your budget.

Next, you can start zeroing in on the size of the property, the location and other features. If you notice that after applying the various filters you are not able to get any properties within your budget, then my recommendation would be to think about what you are willing to compromise on:

1. Can you raise more money so that can buy your ideal property?
2. Are you willing to compromise on space? (E.g. getting a 2-bed house instead of a 3 bed one).
3. Are you willing to compromise on location? (E.g. buying South rather than North of the river, or in Zone 3 rather than Zone 2 in London).
4. Are you willing to compromise on the city? (E.g. buying in Melbourne instead of Sydney, or Wellington instead of

Auckland. This does not necessarily mean that you move to another city, as you may decide to make the purchase as an investment).

5. Are you willing to compromise on the type of property? (E.g. buying a unit or flat instead of a house).

The point is; rather than just sitting and not buying, it is far better to go ahead and make a start. Get on the property ladder so that you do not get left out!

I would recommend that you look at over 100 properties online, on multiple property selling websites to get a feel for the market, i.e. availability of supply, types of properties available, prices by area, characteristics of properties in different areas, etc.

After you have done the above, make a shortlist of the properties that fit your criteria. If you are buying for yourself, then your criteria will be more around the suitability of the property for your needs and so on. If you are an investor, then you will also need to look at other aspects, including potential rental returns, overall financial returns, ease of finding tenants, etc.

Once you have a shortlist of a few properties, say 10 of them, go and physically see them. If you have time and can see a lot more properties, then do that. The more you get out there, see properties and talk to agents and owners, the more you will understand the market and what is out there. The more informed you are, the better the purchase you make will be!

Once you have identified the 2 or 3 properties you may be interested in, you can proceed to make an offer. If it is not an auction, then do not be scared to make an aggressive offer. Clearly if the market is very hot and you are happy to pay a certain price, then offer something close to that so that you are taken seriously but an offer which still leaves some room for negotiation.

If you come across a gem, i.e. you have done some research and you know for a fact that a given property is a great deal then do not waste time. Make an offer and put in the necessary conditions so that you can then perform sufficient due diligence.

Also, if a property looks very reasonably priced, even though for some reason you do not initially feel attracted to it, make sure you at least find out a bit more about it before discarding it from your shortlist.

I still somewhat regret the loss of one of the properties that slipped through my fingers. I was looking at purchasing my third property at that time and was ideally looking for something close to the Mission Bay and Kohimarama area (in the Eastern Bays of Auckland). I saw a property that was very reasonably priced, but its picture and description were not that appealing. So, I did not put the property on my shortlist. However, after spending a couple of weeks and not finding anything interesting, I stumbled across the same house and went to look at it. I could not believe the opportunity and was ready to make an offer there and then. Sadly, I was told that there was already an offer on it and that I could put in a backup offer. Unfortunately, the primary offer went through, and I lost out on this amazing opportunity. I would have probably at least tripled my money on that property by now! C'est la vie, however, a lesson learnt.

CHAPTER 6: HOW TO RAISE MONEY

Given the high price of property, one of the biggest challenges for first time buyers is to raise sufficient equity (or a down payment) in order to get finance.

Raising money is a very *big* question, and I think it is worth spending some time on discussing the fundamentals of managing money. If you can plan and manage your finances, then I can guarantee you will be able to save enough money to buy an appropriate property. At worst, it may not be the home of your dreams and/or it may not be where you want to live, but you will at least be able to get on the property ladder. In time, you would stand a good chance to able to upgrade to the property you truly desire (provided you are also following the rest of the principles outlined in this book).

MANAGING YOUR FINANCES

Step one is to effectively manage your finances. Let us first go through key steps of managing money beyond simply pondering an investment in property:

1. Have overall objectives and a financial plan to fit with those objectives

As highlighted earlier, it really helps to have clear 1-year, 3-year and 5-10-year objectives. E.g. if your objective is to save enough money for a deposit to buy a property in 3 years, make sure you are saving per expectations and that you are tracking the savings. If your plan is based on a higher level of savings than you can currently make based on your income and expenses, then seek ways to increase your income and/or bring down your expenses. If you have clear objectives and a deep desire to achieve these, then doors will open in ways you never expected. Keep the plan up to date and keep adjusting your forecasts, just like any company does.

2. Live within your means and avoid debt, unless it is for very good reasons, e.g. to purchase a property or to study

Most people today live in debt. They live beyond their means. So the first step is to pay off your 'bad' debt as soon as possible before you even think of investing in something else. Otherwise, you will be caught in the vicious cycle of debt and not be able to invest and grow to your full potential. For example, if you have bought a car on debt and are paying 10% interest on it, this is wasted money that could be used as savings for new investments rather than being paid as unnecessary interest to banks.

You may therefore ask the question; how do I pay off my debt if I am not making any more money? See Steps 5 and 6 below for getting rid of your debt and ways to bring your costs down and free up money to pay off your debts.

As noted earlier, I also lived in debt until my mindset changed after I read self-help books and spoke with astute investors. For the past 15 years I have had a simple philosophy — I must aim to save at least 20% of my net income. So, I adjust my lifestyle accordingly, but I also make the best of my money. I find the best deals and I negotiate sensibly — not to the extent of unfairly disadvantaging the other party but ensuring that I am also getting a fair deal. I will give you a practical example of this.

When I was working as an expatriate in Botswana we lived on the Golf Estate in Gaborone city. The Golf Estate was far more expensive than most of the other areas but had a great community and vibe. However, rather than just forking out a tonne of money for the rent, we looked around the estate to find something we liked and that suited our needs, but at the same time was not extravagantly expensive.

We eventually found a nice home with the space and privacy we were looking for. It did not look as extravagant as some of the other houses from the outside, but the interior was amazing. We spared no expense in decorating it and our comfort was no different to most others. We had plenty of space, a beautiful garden, a great pool, etc. yet we paid about 75% of what others did for roughly equivalent houses.

It is a fine balance to have a comfortable life while living within your means and not getting carried away by keeping up with the Joneses. If you can try to keep this balance, then you will find that saving for a property becomes much easier.

3. **Learn to negotiate as this will increase your revenue and bring costs down**

I have dedicated an entire chapter to this topic, as it is very important to be able to negotiate well. See Chapter 15 for further details. I would also strongly recommend that you read some good books on negotiation that go into much more detail on this. I would recommend *The Art of Negotiation* by Michael Wheeler.

4. Have a monthly budget and targeted savings

Everyone needs a sensible monthly budget. A good budget will enable you to have a clear idea of your incomings, outgoings and expected savings.

I would start with what you would like to sensibly save and then use that amount to calculate how much you can spend on a monthly basis. Clearly, if the figure is not realistic then adjust your short-term targeted savings accordingly. In this situation, in order to bring up the savings to the level you desire, you could find ways to increase your income (see point 5 below).

You do not need to be a math whiz or use fancy budget tools. All you need is a simple Excel sheet with your income on one side and your basic expenses on the other side and a short formula that works out your savings. To demonstrate how easy this can be (or should) be, below see an example of this:

MONTHLY NET INCOME			MONTHLY EXPENSES	
Income 1	$4,000		Rent / Mortgage	$2,000
Income 2	$3,500		Groceries	$1,600
Income 2	$1,000		Transport	$200
Total Income	**$8,500**		House Cleaning	$100
			Family Support	$200
			Phone / Mobiles / Internet / TV	$200
			Utilities (Electricity, Water, etc..)	$300
			Car Expenses	$100
			Leisure (diner, cinema, etc.)	$1,000
			Other Shopping (clothes, gifts, etc.)	$200
			Health Related	$100
			Insurances	$100
			Shool Fees	$1,000
			Child Care	$500
			Debt payments and interest	$800
			Total Expenses	**$8,400**

NET SAVINGS PER MONTH	$100

(Total incomme - Total Expenses)

The Budget template in Microsoft Excel is also very good for this. Below is a snapshot of the template:

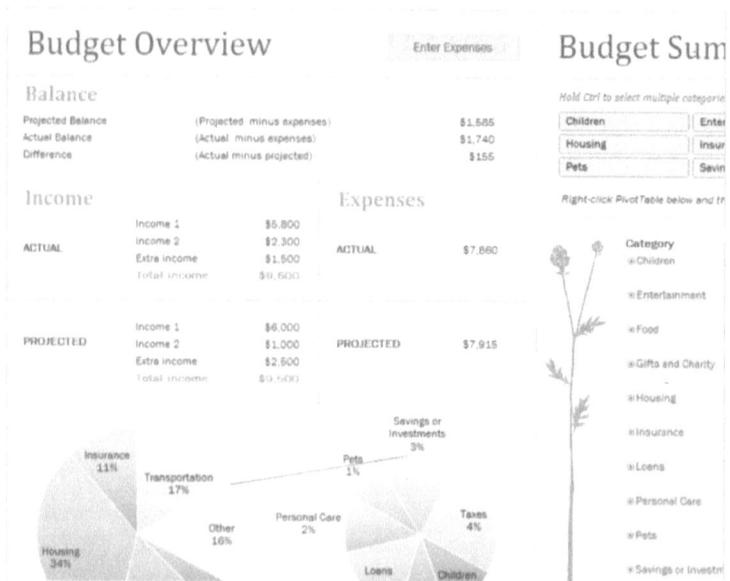

I would highly recommend the book *The Financial Diet* by Chelsea Fagan and Lauren Ver Hage – it proposes a very sensible spending and saving approach based on a 50/30/20 plan.

5. Set aside some funds for emergencies

One thing that is certain is that *life* is uncertain and unpredictable. You never know when you will be hit by unforeseen surprises and will need emergency funds for these, for example; unforeseen health issues, temporary loss of income due to events such as loss of job, or major property repairs.

Rather than being in a fix and having to take on 'bad' debt (which we have already covered is a really bad thing), it is better to be prepared for surprises. Think of a sensible amount and do your best to put that amount aside. Also have insurance (e.g. for income protection) to cover unforeseen events.

6. Find ways to increase your existing income and think of ways to bring in new revenue streams

Even though it may seem like a very difficult task, there are numerous ways to increase your income. You just need to think and look hard enough. Below are some examples of this:

a. Ask for a pay raise or look for a higher-paying job within your own company or in another one. Often you may think that you cannot get a higher salary, but all you have to do is ask or, alternatively, look for a job that pays higher.

When my wife and I first moved to London from New Zealand, the primary reason was for me to do my MBA at London Business School. We had saved enough money to pay my fee outright and we had some savings, but we needed to have an income to sustain our lives during the two years of my MBA. We put together a rough budget, which, converting GBP to NZ dollars, almost made me fall off my chair — particularly the day I realised that a return underground train (tube) ticket would cost me about NZ$18 (or £6) at the time! (It is, of course, well above that in GBP terms now).

Based on our budget, we realised that my wife would have to earn a salary of over a certain amount. Most recruitment agencies told her that the maximum she was likely to get was only about 75% of the minimum figure we had in mind but my wife told them the she had a budget to meet and so she had to find a job paying that salary. Lo and behold, not only did she find a job that paid well over that; she also got it in two weeks and got many other benefits such as free bus and tube transport as part of that role.

If she had listened to the recruitment agencies, then she may have settled for a lower-paying job and simply accepted that it was the maximum amount she could earn at that time!

b. If you have a bonus scheme at work, then ensure that you work hard and smart to maximise your bonus. Many good companies will pay generous bonuses to high performers.

c. Work overtime. Certain roles will allow you to earn more money if you work overtime. If you have this opportunity and want to increase your savings then it is a no brainer make use of it, provided your personal circumstances allow for it.

d. Find a second job in another company or as a self-employed person (e.g. driving an Uber taxi).

One of my relatives drove a taxi for about two years after graduating from university and getting a decent job. The money he made from driving the taxi went straight into his savings account and enabled him to buy his first home. He now has numerous properties and continues to grow his property portfolio.

e. Rent out your home via Airbnb or an equivalent platform while you are on holiday — it is money in the bank!

It is amazing how many homes are empty, gathering dust while people are away on holiday. If you are willing and able to rent out your home while away, the income you make from the rental can pay for part of your holiday!

I have done this time and time again. It all started when we got a pet cat and shortly after had to go for a holiday. We needed to find someone to look after it or put it in a cattery, which would cost us a decent amount of money for two weeks. Somehow, an idea came to mind to rent our flat out on a short-term basis and then add a cheeky little statement in the advert indicating that the flat came with a cat as a bonus to keep the person company. So not only did we get our cat looked after for free, but we made rental money, which covered some of our holiday costs!

If you are renting your property, then your lease — in some cases — may not allow for subletting so make sure you're not breaking any rules. If need be, simply ask your landlord's permission. Share part of the returns if necessary!

f. Write a book on something you are good at and can help others with! (Like I have done in this situation). Read *The Secret of Attracting Money* and *The Law of Attraction Library* by Joe Vitale, which give numerous examples of how you can do this.

In fact, I was reading The Law of Attraction Library as I started writing this book and this truly inspired and motivated me to go ahead with this project!

7. Get rid of your debt

When you are constantly in debt, you are in a vicious cycle of paying more interest, being left with less money, then taking more debt and paying even more interest!

Let us take a simple example here. Imagine you have a personal loan of $10,000 (at 6% interest p.a.), hire purchase items of $3,000 (at 10% interest p.a.) and a constant credit card balance of $5,000 (at 20% interest p.a.). You are, therefore, paying interest per month as follows:

- Personal loan: 5% x 20,000 / 12 = $83
- Hire purchase: 10% x 5,000 / 12 = $42
- Credit card: 20% x 10,000 / 12 = $167
- **Total interest per month = $292**
- **Total interest per year = $3,504**

Now take the scenario where either you do not have any savings per month or your costs are actually higher than your savings. For those of you questioning a situation like this, I can assure you that there is a large percentage of the population in this kind of situation. I found myself in this situation at one stage. You basically end up in a situation per below:

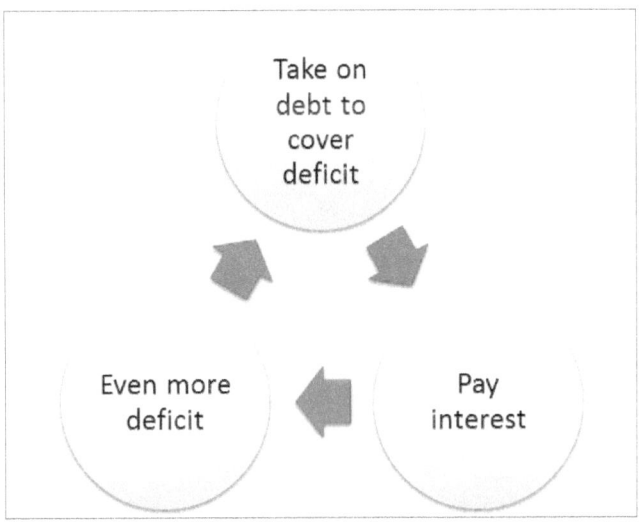

Instead of being in this not-so-attractive situation, you could choose to be in a virtuous cycle of investment, getting more returns, then investing more and further multiplying your returns

Take the scenario where you save $500 per month. Even if you get only a 3% return, by the end of the year, you would have made almost $100 in interest earnings (inclusive of the compounding of interest) so you would have a total saving of almost $6,100 at the end of the year. In 10 years you would have saved over $70,000, inclusive of over $10,000 in interest earnings. This is a very simple example and with low returns; however, if you put your savings into investments, such as property, then your money will multiply beyond what you can imagine, and you may even find yourself a millionaire in a few years' time if you continue to astutely re-invest your returns.

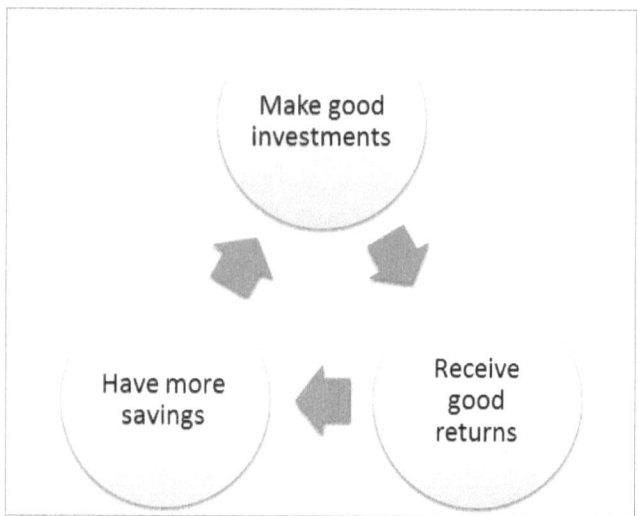

However hard it may feel, there are many ways to get rid of your debt. All it takes is to have a strong desire and determination. Below are some ways to reduce and/or entirely eliminate your debt:

a. The first step is to avoid any new debt, otherwise the interest on your new debt will further prevent you from getting rid of your existing debt and you will remain in a vicious cycle. This means that you may have to hold off certain purchases and reduce your expenses.

b. Sell items you do not need and free up some cash to pay off your debt (e.g. the guitar or golf clubs that you haven't touched in the past five years, or the extra TV you bought for your bedroom and hardly use!).

c. Return the items that you bought on debt if possible (e.g. if you are still within the period of 'acceptable returns'). Alternatively, sell the items if you are struggling to pay for them, e.g. if your new car is taking up a massive chunk of your income.

d. Explore if there is a way to negotiate the interest costs down or find out if there is another lender who is willing to give you debt at a lower interest. This will enable you to reduce your cost of debt and use the savings to pay it down quicker — one option here is to consolidate all your debt with one provider (e.g. interest rates on personal loans can be far lower than interest rates on store cards). Banks are advertising this all the time!

I personally did this at one stage where I had debt on two different credit cards and on a store card. I was paying as high as 24% interest at that time! Thankfully my bank proposed to me to get a personal loan to consolidate all my debt and if I recall well, I was paying interest of about 7% or 8% at that time. This was far better than the 24%! After I paid off my personal loan, I never took another loan again! I actually have three credit cards from different countries, but I always pay off any expenses within the forty-day interest-free period and so I never incur any interest expenses.

Credit cards can actually be a great tool as they give you 'working capital' to fund a good chunk of your monthly expenses. Additionally, you get other benefits such as cashback or air miles. However, the key is to pay off the statement balance before the interest free period expires (i.e. by the due date indicated on your monthly statement). You need to be really disciplined and ensure that you do not fall in the trap of using your credit card as free money and then end up in the same cycle of debt. If you think that you do not have enough self-control in this regard, then it is better to return all your credit cards!

e. See help from a professional debt negotiation or debt management company such as American Consumer Credit Counselling (www.consumercredit.com) in the US, Debt Advisory Centre (www.debtadvisorycenture.co.uk) in the UK, Debt Solvers (www.debt.solvers.com.au) in Australia and Ooraa (http://www.ooraa.org/NZ/) in New Zealand. Ooraa also provides services in the US, Canada and Australia. A quick Google search should give you information on relevant debt management or debt negotiation services provides in your own location.

f. Cut down your existing costs to free up some cash to pay off your debt. A big way to save money is by renting a cheaper place for a little while. You may have to compromise on space or location, but it will be well worth it once your debts are paid off and you enter a virtuous cycle of saving. There are many other ways of cutting costs, e.g. reducing transport costs, shopping at cheaper supermarkets, skipping a holiday trip (or taking a cheaper option), etc.

See **Point 8** below for further details on this.

In fact, if you are in debt and are looking to reduce it, then I urge you to take a pen and paper and make a list of areas where you could cut cost starting *now*!

g. Ask family for help to pay off debt and, even if you need to pay them back, at least you will not have to pay interest. It is better to put your ego aside and ask for help if someone can help you. You never know — once you are in a healthy financial position, you may be able to return the same favour!

h. Get legal advice about potential insolvency / bankruptcy if you are in severe debt and have no ability to get out of it.

i. Consult a personal budget or financial advisor if you need further help with getting rid of your debt. Below are some examples:

- The National Association of Personal Financial Advisors – NAPFA (https://www.napfa.org) in the US
- The Money Advice Service (www.moneyadviceservice.org.uk) in the UK
- My Budget (www.mybudget.com.au) in Australia
- Family Budgeting (www.familybudgeting.org.nz) in New Zealand

8. Constantly try to find ways to bring down your existing costs (while not necessarily reducing your lifestyle)

This was briefly covered in the earlier point of reducing your debt, but we will expand on this here.

The idea here is not to be a penny pincher and to be 'penny wise and pound foolish'. However, whether you are an individual or the largest organisation in this world, you must watch your costs, otherwise they can spiral out of control. There are always ways to sensibly cut costs without sacrificing your quality of life.

Additionally, there is no reason to cut costs just for the sake of it. Cost-cutting should be done mainly where you feel there is room for improvement and where you could do with better savings. In fact, if you get into the best practice of managing and keeping a close eye on your costs, this will become a natural part of your way of life. If you have sufficient wealth then you can spend as you wish and enjoy the quality of life you want (e.g. buying the best cars, buying or renting the best houses, etc.)

When you really want to cut your costs, there are numerous ways to do this. Again, all it takes is some thought and discipline. You can literally start by making a list and taking action now! Below are some potential areas of reducing cost:

a. **Reduce your rent.** Rent is one of your biggest costs and hence the first target area to assess whether there is any room for potential savings. There are numerous ways to do this. You could downsize your home for a certain period, move to a cheaper location, get a flat mate, live with your parents or other family for a while, re-negotiate your rent, etc. Yes, you may have to compromise on your desired quality of life, but I can assure you that it would only be for a certain period of time until you have strengthened your financial position. The key is to get out of the vicious cycle and move into the virtuous cycle!

b. **Cut your grocery expenses** by buying at a cheaper supermarket and ensuring that you take advantage of any discounts and/or promotions. Also, be sure to reduce any wastage! More on this later.

c. **Reduce your transport costs**, e.g. by riding or walking to work. You could also use a kick scooter! This will not only save you money but keep you healthy and possibly eliminate your gym costs!

d. **Reduce discretionary expenses**, e.g. buy drinks from a supermarket or bottle store and have these at home with friends rather than going out to expensive bars and clubs (and then also having the cost of a taxi ride at the end of the night), watch a movie at home instead of going to cinemas, etc.

e. **Reduce schooling costs where appropriate**. For example, private school fees can vary substantially and sometimes certain government schools (e.g. Grammar schools in the UK) can provide very good education standards.

f. **Buy second-hand items where possible**. There are numerous items that can be purchased second hand without compromising the utility or the benefit you get from the item.

Let us say you are looking for a new TV. Often you will find a better-quality TV at a cheaper price if you buy second-hand rather than purchasing a lower-quality, brand new one.

E.g. I just checked the price of a 47-inch LG Smart TV on eBay and the price of a brand new one is £400 and a pre-owned one in excellent condition is £300. That is 25% of the value saved for the same item.

I recently bought a top-of the line laptop retailing at around £800 for £400 simply because it was an ex-demo version. It was literally like new and yet I got it pretty much at half price. I also just bought a virtually new top-of-the-line iPhone X at 20% discount because it had been used barely for a week.

The same applies to many other types of electronic items.

Children's clothes can be another area of savings. Children tend to quickly grow out of their clothes and you will often find almost new (and in some cases completely new) clothes at a throw-away price on websites like eBay and Trademe.

In my view, one should not even think about buying a brand-new car as you lose as much as 20% of its value in the first year. Why not buy an almost new car that is, say, one to three years old and in very good condition and save yourself as much as 50% of cost?

Imagine if a new car costs $40,000 and you buy it on finance. After the first year, the value of the car will be around $32,000. Yet you may find that, despite the first year's finance repayment, the value of the car will be less than what you owe the bank. You will therefore be in a situation of negative equity. You would easily buy the same car second hand and save yourself this steep drop of value and the situation of being in negative equity.

At the time of writing this book, a basic specification BMW 320i was worth $72,000 in New Zealand. A one-year old high spec BMW 320i M Sport model was for $59,900. There were numerous others in the same price range, so this was not an exception. So you could save 17% and get a higher spec car.

Of course, if you have the money and you are willing to spend it; go for the brand new one and have the whole experience of buying a new car with your own specifications. However, if you are trying to save money, why buy a new car when you get serious value for money by buying a 1 or 2-year old car — or an even older one where appropriate?

g. **Research before making any large purchases.** Whenever I make a large purchase, e.g. a new electronic item, car, etc. I make sure that I do tonnes of research and use cost comparison websites. It is incredible how costs can vary among different sellers and by simply going online and doing some research you can often easily save yourself 10%-20% of cost.

h. **Buy online whenever possible and appropriate**. Online companies have lower overheads as they do not need to pay high street rents, their staffing costs are lower, etc. So they can sell their items cheaper than stores. I often do most of my purchases online. Modern day, you can also buy clothes online if you trust the seller and the brands. If the clothes do not fit, you can simply return them for a full refund. I love CK suits and often buy these online as I already know the fit and size that is perfect for me.

However, be wary of people wanting to rip you off. *I was recently looking for a kick scooter and found a brand and model I really liked. On the official website of the company, the scooter was about £125. The same scooter was being sold for £175 on eBay!* **Just because something is being sold on eBay (or a similar site) does not mean that it is the cheapest option! Make sure that you do your homework.**

i. Borrow items where possible. There are numerous situations where you could easily borrow an item from family, friends or colleagues where you desperately need the item, but the same item is using up storage space in someone else's house! Sometimes you actually do the person a favour by borrowing or taking the item from them. All you have to do is ask around!

When we were living in Botswana, we had a decent-sized garden and needed a lawn mower after ours broke down. We were going to purchase a new one as we could easily afford it but one of my wife's friends told us that they were not using theirs as they did not have a lawn in their new home. So we ended up borrowing that for a few months and saved ourselves the unnecessary cost of buying a new one.

j. Hand-me-downs. If you already have more than one child or are planning to, you can save a whole lot of cost by keeping clothes and toys and handing these down to the younger ones. You can even look to your extended family and friends for hand-me-downs as it not only saves money but saves the planet by avoiding wastage!

k. Ask yourself if you really need to buy something and whether it can wait for later. We always want the latest gadgets (I, for one, do) and sometimes we simply need to ask ourselves whether the money would be better spent somewhere else.

    I had a BMW X5 (you can probably tell by now that I am a big fan of BMWs!) and after it was around 6 years old, I was thinking of upgrading to a newer model. It was going to cost me around £30,000 to do that. My X5 was in perfect condition but I was really attracted to the new model. I even flew to a different city to view a car I had seen advertised. I did not buy the car but the person selling it ended up becoming a good friend! At the same time, I wanted to extend my property portfolio and I asked myself what would add more value. At the end of the day I decided against the purchase and instead put the money towards making extensions to 2 of my properties. These extensions not only added substantial value to the houses but also helped increase their rents, thus increasing my passive income.

l. Avoid wastage, e.g. food. How often do you end up buying too much of something and then throwing it away, for example, when it sits at the back of your fridge or pantry? If you are a typical consumer, then I can bet that you do this numerous times every year! Each and every item you throw out cost you money that you had to work hard for. In essence, you are throwing away what you sweated for. Buy less, do not overstock and make use of what you have rather than buying new items. This sounds very simple but how many of us follow this? I have to remind myself of this frequently as I also fall into the same trap!

If you read the best-selling book *The Diet Myth* by Tim Spector, you will find that a lot of food we throw away because it is supposedly expired is a complete waste. I, for one, no longer throw away food purely due to its expiry date. However, rather than taking my word for it, I would encourage you to read this book. It totally opened my mind on many topics!

m. Look after things and make them last so you do not have to waste money buying them again, e.g. if you have good clothes make sure that you wash or dry clean them per recommendation and store them well so that they continue to look good longer and have a longer life overall.

n. Take advantage of sales and promotions — where possible, buy items on sale, even if you do not need them immediately but know that you will need them later.

This is how I buy many of my clothes. I love brands such as Boss and Hackett. Whenever I see a big sale of these brands, I have a look and if I fancy something, I buy it. This way I never run out of good clothes and I end up paying 20% to 50% less than retail price. I have an Italian friend from Genoa. For anyone who knows Italians, he is a true 'Genoese'! He is a highly paid, high-flying management consultant and although he wears amazing designer clothes, he never buys any of them at retail price — he always manages to find incredible discounts, sometimes up to 80%!

o. Negotiate! Whenever possible, negotiate when you make any purchase. Even when things appear to be fixed-price, there can be a chance to negotiate. If you do not ask, then you do not get. Simple as that. Negotiation is a big topic in its own right and I have hence dedicated an entire section to it later in the book.

p. Where possible, buy good quality things (even if they are second hand) as they will last longer, look/feel better and ultimately cost you less. *If I have a limited budget I would rather buy a decent second-hand TV or HiFi system, rather than a new, lower-quality model. Also, I prefer buying quality clothes and having fewer items rather than having lots of cheap clothes that do not look and feel as good and do not last as long. I learned to do this from a number of self-help books that I read many years back.*

9. Protect your assets and other belongings through insurance

You must have insurance to cover any damage to your property. If your property is rented, then be sure that your insurance coverage is appropriate for a rental property. Also get insurance for your key belongings, such as expensive electronic items and jewellery. Imagine you just paid £1,000 for the latest iPhone and you then end up losing it or someone steals it! If it is insured through a decent insurance company, you should get your money back (or your item replaced) in no time.

A key tip here is also to not go with cheap insurance companies. They are cheap for a reason! You may find that pay-outs could take much longer, or your claim could be outright declined due to some small text that you did not read!

Additionally, if you have a rental property, consider getting rental protection insurance in case you incur any rental arrears or the tenants damage your property.

BORROWING MONEY FROM THE BANKS

Once you have your finances under control, the next step is to borrow money for your investment.

All banks want to make money. Lending money is a key method through which they do this. However, banks want to manage their risk and meet the ever-more-stringent regulatory requirements. As a property buyer or investor, you want to position yourself as a safe bet for the bank. You will need to show that you have sufficient and reliable income (in other words you have a decent job or business), a history of saving (i.e. your down payment did not magically appear in your account) and stability (i.e. you have not been moving around from place to place for no good reason). There may also be other special conditions, such as your country of residence and the country where the property is located. Banks generally do not like to lend money for property purchases in foreign countries.

If you can tick these boxes, then you will make yourself an attractive client to the banks. Otherwise, you will have a tough time convincing the banks to lend to you.

Prior to the 2007-2008 financial crisis, banks were willing to lend to anyone; however, times have changed, and banks have been forced to become far more risk averse, not only due to economic realities, but also due to regulation. There are even tougher rules for purchasing a property if you already own one or more properties, e.g. in New Zealand you require a 40% deposit.

When I was initially living in London (prior to my placement in Botswana), I was very easily able to find finance for the flat I purchased there. When I left for Botswana I informed my bank I was going to be out of the country for some time and they gave me a concession to rent the flat while I was away. I was able to get this concession on a yearly basis for three years but after that the bank told me that they would no longer be able to continue with this concession and that I would need to take on a 'buy to let' mortgage. I therefore duly applied for this but was surprised to find that the bank would not give me this mortgage as I lived in a country they did not lend to — although the actual property was in the UK! I was as safe a client as one could get but just because of the country of my residence the bank would not lend to me. Go figure!

I was a bit disappointed, but I did not think it was a big deal as many other banks would potentially lend to me. I called at least twenty banks only to find that none of them were willing to lend to me for one reason or another. It took me months to finally find a single willing bank through a broker and I had to incur substantial set-up costs to move my mortgage.

This whole episode taught me a lesson not to take lending for granted and to really understand the expectations of banks and how any country moves in your life can have substantial impact on your borrowings.

BRIDGING LOANS / SECONDARY MORTGAGES

There are banks and other financial institutions that will be willing to finance a property through a bridging loan or secondary mortgage. However, these tend to be expensive and their objective is to serve as a short-term solution (e.g. if you are buying a new replacement property while your existing property is still on the market).

GOVERNMENT SCHEMES AND GRANTS

There are a number of government schemes and grants targeted at first home buyers or lower income families.

US SCHEMES

According to USA.gov, below are the schemes in the US for first time home buyers (Help Buying a New Home, n.d.)

The Federal Housing Administration (FHA) for First-Time Homebuyers

The Department of Housing and Urban Development (HUD) has two programs to make home buying more affordable:

1. **FHA Loans:** For first-time buyers, the requirements are not as strict compared to other loans. Eligibility is as below:

   - Cash down payment, or the deposit, can be as low as 3.5% of the purchase price.
   - Your credit score doesn't need to be as high as in the case of conventional loans.
   - Closing costs may be partly covered or lower than conventional loans.

2. **HUD Home:** HUD takes ownership of properties when owners default on their FHA mortgage. These properties are known as HUD homes or HUD Real Estate Owned (REO) property.

   Eligibility depends on your credit score and having an approved mortgage. You can also use an FHA mortgage to buy a HUD home.

Homeownership Vouchers

If your family has a low-income or lives in public housing, the Department of Housing and Urban Development (HUD) Homeownership Voucher Program can provide you help with monthly mortgage payments and other home expenses.

To be eligible you must:

- be a first-time buyer per HUD's requirements
- meet a minimum income requirement as defined by the local Public Housing Agencies (PHAs)
- have at least one adult working full-time for a minimum of one year
- complete the homeownership and housing counselling program

Other Programmes in the US

The USA.gov website lists the following additional programmes to help people buy properties:

- Indian Home Loan Guarantee Program
- Programs for Service Members and Veterans
- Programs for Rural Residents
- State Programs
- Foreclosure Properties

UK SCHEMES

Below are key UK schemes for first time buyers (GOV.UK, 2017)

Help to Buy Equity Loan

To be eligible for this loan, the home you buy must:

- be a new-build home
- not cost more than £600,000 in England (or £300,000 in Wales)
- be the only one you own
- not be sub-let or rented out after you buy it
- be one that you can show you can't afford (if you're applying in Wales)

How it works:

- you need a 5% deposit
- the government will lend you up to 20% (up to 40% in London)
- you need a mortgage of up to 75% for the rest (up to 55% in London)
- You must buy your home from a registered 'Help to Buy' builder - your agent should have a list.

For example, if you are buying a home worth £500,000 outside of London and have a 5% deposit, the breakdown of the figures would be as follows:

	Amount	Percentage
Your investment	£25,000	5%
Government equity loan	£100,000	20%
Mortgage	£375,000	75%

For a purchase in London, the figures would be as below:

	Amount	Percentage
Your investment	£25,000	5%
Government equity loan	£200,000	40%
Mortgage	£275,000	55%

Equity loan fees:

You'll have to pay equity loan fees, but not for the first five years.

In the sixth year, you'll be charged a fee of 1.75% of the loan's value. The fee then increases every year, according to the Retail Prices Index (RPI) plus 1%. (E.g. if RPI is 2% then your fee will increase by 3% so in the 7th year your fee will be 1.8025% due to the 3% increase in fee)

It is worth noting that the fees don't count towards paying back the loan.

Paying back the loan:

You must pay back the loan after 25 years, or when you sell your home — whichever comes first. The amount you pay back depends on how much your home is worth (the market value). For example:

Market Value of Home	Equity Loan	Amount
Bought for £500,000	20%	Borrowed £100,000
Sold for £600,000	20%	Pay back £120,000

You can pay back all, or part of, your equity loan at any time. The smallest repayment is 10% of the market value of your home.

You can apply for the loan through a 'Help to Buy' agent. Visit https://www.gov.uk/affordable-home-ownership-schemes/help-to-buy-equity-loan for further details.

Help to Buy ISA

If you're saving to buy your first home, the government will top up your savings by 25% (up to £3,000). If you're buying with someone else, they can also get a Help to Buy ISA. You don't have to pay back the top up provided by the government.

In terms of eligibility, the home you buy must:

- have a purchase price of up to £250,000 (or up to £450,000 in London)
- be the only home you own
- be where you intend to live

The good news is that you can use the scheme with an equity loan.

Examples of government top up payments (per annum) are as follows:

Your Savings	Government Payments	Total
£1,600 (minimum)	£400	£2,000
£8,000	£2,000	£10,000
£12,000 (maximum)	£3,000	£15,000

You can apply through various banks. Refer to the website https://www.gov.uk/affordable-home-ownership-schemes/help-to-buy-isa for further details.

Shared Ownership

You can get a shared ownership home through a housing association. You buy a share of your home (between 25% and 75%) and pay rent on the rest.

There are different rules in Northern Ireland and Scotland. You will need to contact your local authority to find out about buying a shared ownership home in Wales.

In terms of eligibility, you can buy a home through shared ownership if your household earns £80,000 a year or less (or £90,000 a year or less in London) and any of the following apply:

- you're a first-time buyer
- you used to own a home, but can't afford to buy one now
- you're an existing shared owner

Special Conditions for older people and those with disabilities

- If you are aged 55 or over, you can buy up to 75% of your home through the Older People's Shared Ownership (OPSO) scheme. Once you own 75% you do not need to pay rent on the rest.
- You can apply for a scheme called 'home ownership for people with a long-term disability' (HOLD) if other Help-to-Buy scheme properties don't meet your needs, for example, if you need a ground-floor property. With this scheme you can buy up to 25% of your home. If you are disabled, you can also apply for the general shared ownership scheme and own up to 75% of your home.

Buying more shares

- You can buy more of your home after you become the owner. This is known as "staircasing".

- The cost of your new share will depend on how much your home is worth when you want to buy the share.
- The housing association will get your property valued and let you know the cost of your new share. You'll have to pay the valuer's fee.

Selling your home

- If you own a share of your home, the housing association has the right to buy it first. This is known as 'first refusal'. The housing association also has the right to find a buyer for your home.
- If you own 100% of your home, you can sell it yourself.

AUSTRALIA SCHEMES

First Home Owner Grant

The First Home Owner Grant (FHOG) scheme was introduced on 1 July 2000 to offset the effect of the GST on home ownership. It is a national scheme funded by the states and territories and administered under their own legislation. Under the scheme, a one-off grant is payable to first home owners that satisfy all the eligibility criteria. (firsthome.gov.au, 2017).

Different states have different levels of grants, e.g. The Queensland First Home Owners' Grant is a state government initiative to help first home owners to get their new first home sooner. Depending on the date of your contract, you'll get $15,000 or $20,000 towards buying or building your new house, unit or townhouse (valued at less than $750,000) (firsthomeowners.initiatives.qld.gov.au, 2017).

First Home Super Saver Scheme

A new scheme was announced by the Australian federal government in its 2017 budget. According to the Government's budget website:

"From 1 July 2017, individuals can make voluntary contributions of up to $15,000 per year and $30,000 in total, to their superannuation account to purchase a first home. These contributions, which are taxed at 15 per cent, along with deemed earnings, can be withdrawn for a deposit. Withdrawals will be taxed at marginal tax rates less a 30 per cent offset and allowed from 1 July 2018.

For most people, the First Home Super Saver Scheme could boost the savings they can put towards a deposit by at least 30 per cent compared with saving through a standard deposit account. This is due to the concessional tax treatment and the higher rate of earnings often realised within superannuation.

Many employees will be able to take advantage of salary sacrifice arrangements to make pre-tax contributions.

Individuals who are self-employed, or whose employers do not offer salary sacrifice, can claim a tax deduction on personal contributions, meaning savings effectively come out of pre-tax income.

Voluntary contributions under this scheme must be made within existing superannuation caps. The total concessional contributions an individual can make, from both compulsory employer contributions and voluntary contributions, including those made under the scheme cannot exceed $25,000 in 2017-18." (Australian Fedebral Budget, 2017-2018)

NEW ZEALAND SCHEMES

Below are the details per the New Zealand Government website (www.gov.nz, 2017)

KiwiSaver HomeStart grant

If you're a first-time buyer and you've been making regular KiwiSaver contributions for at least 3 years, you may be able to apply for a KiwiSaver HomeStart grant through Housing New Zealand.

How it works

If you buy an existing home, you can get $1,000 for each year you've paid into the scheme. The most you can get is $5,000 for 5 years.

If you buy a new home or land, you can get $2,000 for each year you've paid into the scheme. The most you can get is $10,000 for 5 years.

If you buy a property with other people who qualify for a KiwiSaver HomeStart grant, you can all apply but the most you can get for one property is:

- $10,000 for an existing property
- $20,000 if you buy a new home or land for a new home.

Who can apply?

To apply, you must:

- be 18 or older
- have been contributing at least the minimum amount of your income (currently 3%) to your KiwiSaver scheme for 3 years
- have had an income in the previous 12 months (before tax) of less than:
    o $85,000 for 1 person
    o $130,000 for 2 or more people

- have a deposit of at least 10% of the purchase price
- agree to live in your property for at least 6 months:
    - From the date you buy your home (the settlement date), or
    - If the house is new, from when the code compliance certificate is issued.

See website http://www.hnzc.co.nz/ways-we-can-help-you-to-own-a-home/firsthome/

KIWISAVER FIRST HOME WITHDRAWAL

You can apply to withdraw your KiwiSaver savings to put towards buying your first home if you've belonged to your KiwiSaver scheme for at least 3 years. You can withdraw your savings, but you must leave at least $1,000 in your KiwiSaver account.

See website http://www.hnzc.co.nz/ways-we-can-help-you-to-own-a-home/kiwisaver-homestart-grant-and-savings-withdrawal/kiwisaver-first-home-withdrawal/

WELCOME HOME LOAN

With a Welcome Home Loan, you might be able to get a home loan if you only have a 10% deposit. How much you can borrow depends on where you live in New Zealand and what you can afford.

Welcome Home Loan

You get a Welcome Home Loan from a bank or other lender — not all banks and lenders offer this option. Housing New Zealand underwrites the loan. Before you can get a loan, you need to meet criteria set by the government and your lender.

For the government to approve your loan, you must:

- have a 10% deposit
- buy a house that costs no more than the maximum price for your region — the regional cap
- have income before tax in the last 12 months of no more than:
    - $85,000 per year if you're single
    - $130,000 per year if 2 or more of you are buying a house together.

Welcome Home Loan — am I eligible?

Contact your lender to find out their conditions for a Welcome Home Loan. They could consider:

- whether or not they think you can repay the loan
- your credit history
- any debts you have
- your banking history

See website http://www.welcomehomeloan.co.nz/

IF YOU ARE A MAORI

You can get money to build, buy or relocate a home on your ancestral land.

See the website: http://www.hnzc.co.nz/ways-we-can-help-you-to-own-a-home/kainga-whenua/kainga-whenua-loans-for-individuals/

HELP TO BUY A HOUSE OWNED BY HOUSING NEW ZEALAND (FirstHome GRANT)

In some areas of New Zealand, you can buy a property that Housing New Zealand no longer needs. First-home buyers can apply for a FirstHome grant of up to $20,000 towards the deposit needed to buy one of these properties.

If you're an existing tenant in a state house, you can buy your home if it is available for purchase.

See website http://www.hnzc.co.nz/ways-we-can-help-you-to-own-a-home/firsthome/

RAISING MONEY THROUGH OTHER SOURCES

There are times that banks will either not be willing to lend to you at all, or not agree to lend the total amount you require. Rather than giving up on the potential purchase, it is worth pursuing other fund-raising options. Some are harder than what you would expect, but others may turn out to be far easier than what you thought. This will entirely depend on your personal circumstances and the nature of your network.

1. Borrow from family and/or friends.
2. Co-invest with family and/or friends.
3. Co-invest with other like-minded investors.
4. Get vendor finance (e.g. paying through instalments).
5. Get peer-to-peer lending. This is a growing industry and provides an alternative way for people to raise money rather than going via traditional banks. This could be the future of how everyone borrows money. The money comes from those who want to invest and get more decent returns than fixed deposits but to still have a lower level risk compared to investing in shares.

Below are examples of some of these platforms:

- House Crowd (www.thehousecrowd.com)
- Simple Backing (www.simplebacking.co.uk)
- Venture Crowd (www.venturecrowd.com.au)
- CrowdFundUP (www.crowdfundup.com)
- BrickRaise (www.crunchbase.com)
- Lending Club (www.lendingclub.com)
- Prosper (www.prosper.com)

Real estate crowd funding is in its infancy stages globally, particularly in Australia and NZ. In fact, I did not come across any real estate crowd funding site in New Zealand at the time of writing this book.

6. Get short term or bridging finance through specialist providers such as https://www.lendinvest.com/ (they not only provide finance for new purchases but also for refurbishments and developments)

When I purchased one of my properties, I was short of about $20,000 of equity, based on the lending rules at that time. I had come across an incredible property (actually it was my wife, as usual, who had found us this great investment) and I did not want to lose it. I therefore tried to investigate other options to raise this $20,000. And then an idea sprung to mind. There was a lovely secretary who worked for us and she was close to retirement, so I knew that she would have sufficient savings. I approached her and asked her if I could borrow the $20,000 for a short period of 6 months and give her a 10% return (double what the banks were offering at the time). Given that she knew me and trusted me and given that the return was attractive, she happily lent me the money. And within 6 months I was able to fully refund this money along with the interest of $1,000 (i.e. 10% annual interest pro-rated to 6 months). I, in fact, did not need to use my own money *because within 6 months the property value had gone up and the bank was willing to give me the extra $20k lending!*

I also recently acquired a piece of land close to a pristine beach. Unfortunately, the banks would not lend me money for it as it was an international investment and I did not have sufficient cash to pay for it up front. I used 2 of the earlier stated alternative-financing options to still buy the property:

1. *I approached a close friend to buy the land in partnership.*
2. *I agreed vendor finance for us to pay the purchase price in 3 instalments over a period of 1 year.*

The moral of the above stories is that you do not have to give up on the purchase of a good property simply because banks are not willing to lend you the full amount. There are other options to explore!

CHAPTER 7: MEASURING THE RETURN ON INVESTMENT

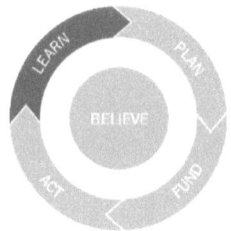

It is very important to know the return you will get on any investment in order to get maximum returns from your funds and other resources (e.g. your time). For example, if you have two different properties you could buy, putting emotion aside, how would you objectively determine which is the better investment? Neither individuals nor organisation have unlimited funds to invest, so you must have a practical way of determining where to invest your capital.

I will do my best to give you some basic principles on measuring return on investment so that you can get an appreciation for the different methods and do some basic computations.

You can google any of the methods and you will get a lot more detail and examples in case you want to dig deeper in this area. Alternatively, if you are interested in learning further about this in a more structured way, I would strongly recommend that you find relevant books (e.g. *The Portable MBA in Finance and Accounting* by Theodore Grossman) and/or courses dedicated to this topic.

BASIC RETURN ON INVESTMENT (ROI) APPROACH

The simplest way to measure return on investment is to determine what your annual return is and to divide that by the initial investment amount.

Let us take a very simple example. Imagine you invest $100,000 into a business and your annual net returns after all expenses are $10,000.

- Initial investment = $100,000
- Annual net return = $10,000
- ROI = Annual net return / Initial investment = $10,000 / $100,000 = 10%

However, this approach is very simplistic and does not take into account the duration of the investment and any variability in returns. In my view it is a quick and dirty way to determine the rough return on a potential investment.

PAYBACK PERIOD

Payback period is another very simple way of assessing the attractiveness of an investment. It basically computes how long it takes for an investment to pay for itself. In essence, you only start making a profit on your investment once the initial investment has been paid off. The disadvantages of this method are that it does not take the time value of money into consideration and also does not take into consideration the returns after the payback period. However, it can serve as a good rough guide to assess different investments and to determine which investment will pay itself off fastest.

INTERNAL RATE OF RETURN (IRR) APPROACH

The IRR approach is a more sophisticated way of determining a percentage return on investment. It allows for variable investment and return amounts over a pre-determined period of time and also takes the time value of money into consideration, i.e. a 10% return two years from now is not the same as a 10% return today.

Let us take a simple example where you have the potential to invest $100,000 in a business and expect net returns of $10,000 in years 1 to 3, $20,000 in years 4 to 7 and $30,000 in years 8-10.

We enter these numbers in Excel (or an equivalent programme as below) and then use the IRR function to compute the return of 12% as below.

	Year 1	Year 2	Year 3	Year 4	Year 5	Year 6	Year 7	Year 8	Year 9	Year 10	Total
Investment	-100,000										-100,000
Net return	10,000	10,000	10,000	20,000	20,000	20,000	20,000	30,000	30,000	30,000	200,000
IRR	12.0%										

If you used the basic ROI approach, the average return would be 20%, as computed below:

- Average annual return = $200,000/10 = $20,000
- Basic ROI = $20,000 / $100,000 = 20%

So we see that using the IRR gives us a far more accurate indication of the return (12% compared to the 20% using the basic method), as it takes the time value of money into consideration. The reason the IRR figure is lower is because the higher cash flows come at a later time (i.e. the returns are $10,000 in years 1 to 3 and then eventually increase to $20,000 in years 5-7 and then to $30,000 in years 8-10). If the returns were evenly spread as $20,000 per year, then the IRR approach would also give a return of 20%.

I hope the above makes sense. However, if it does not, do not worry. All you have to do is to plug in the numbers into Excel and use the IRR formula to compute the returns for you. There are tonnes of examples online if you want to learn more about this and see other worked examples.

NET PRESENT VALUE (NPV) APPROACH

The NPV approach is slightly different to the IRR approach in that it determines a cash value figure by applying a 'Weighted Average Cost of Capital' (WACC) factor to the cash flows.

As explained earlier, "Cost of capital refers to the opportunity cost of making a specific investment. It is the rate of return that could have been earned by putting the same money into a different investment with equal risk. Thus, the cost of capital is the rate of return required to persuade the investor to make a given investment."

Computing the cost of capital is a complex process and has some subjective components, which can have a big impact on the figure. The riskier the investment, the higher the cost of capital, as you would expect a higher return for a riskier investment. The amount of equity versus debt in a given investment also has impact on the cost of capital (in general; the higher the debt, the lower the cost of capital).

The basic formula to compute the WACC is as below:

WACC = (Percent Equity x Cost of Equity) + ((Percent Debt x Cost of Debt) x (1 – Tax Rate))

Let us take a simple example. If you are buying a property worth $500,000 and will put in $100,000 of your own cash and borrow $400,000 at 4% interest, then:

- Percent Equity = $100,000/$500,000 = 20%
- Percent Debt = $400,000/$500,000 = 80%
- Cost of Debt = 5%
- Tax Rate = 30% (assumed figure — you would apply your marginal tax rate here, i.e. the top category of the tax you pay)
- Cost of Equity = the minimum return you would expect on your cash investment. This figure needs to take account of the level of risk of the property and there are complex formulas to compute this, mainly for commercial investments.

  However, I tend to use a rule of thumb figure of at least double the return I would get from putting my money in a fixed interest rate account, as investing in property is riskier than putting your money in a fixed savings account. For very low-risk investments in developed countries, I tend to use 5% and in developing countries, I tend to use a figure of around 10%. In this case, let us assume a figure of 10% for simplicity

- WACC = (20% x 10%) + ((80% x 5%) x (1 – 30%) = 4.8%

If we take the same cash flow example as in the case of the IRR approach and assume a cost of capital of 4.8% (per the above calculation) the return would be computed as below:

	Year 1	Year 2	Year 3	Year 4	Year 5	Year 6	Year 7	Year 8	Year 9	Year 10	Total
Investment	-100,000										-100,000
Net return	10,000	10,000	10,000	20,000	20,000	20,000	20,000	30,000	30,000	30,000	200,000
NPV	48,298										

In essence this tells us that the NPV of your investment is $10,784. Any figure above 0 is a good investment, as it makes at least the return you expect based on the cost of capital.

If you want to pick between different potential investments, you could compute the NPV of each and pick the one that has the highest return.

CHAPTER 8: HOW TO MAKE AN OFFER AND EXECUTE THE PROPERTY PURCHASE

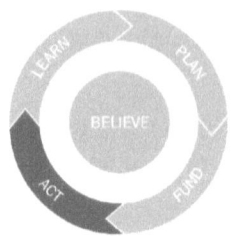

FINDING A GOOD LAWYER OR SOLICITOR

It is critical that you find a good lawyer (solicitor) to help you with the property purchase or the conveyancing process. They can advise you on all sorts of aspects, including the property sale and purchase agreement (if there are any modifications to the standard agreement).

The UK Law Society describes conveyancing as "the legal transfer of property (from seller to buyer)". How long it takes depends on several things, such as how many buyers and sellers are involved in the process, but it can take weeks or months.

Key responsibilities of the solicitor include:

1. Helping demystify the property purchase and explaining the whole process to you, step by step.
2. Carrying out searches on the property and its title to ensure that you know as much about it as possible and there are no surprises (e.g. the property lying in a flood risk area or any monies being owed on the property).

3. Entering into contract, or (in other words), completion of a sales and purchase agreement. This includes confirmation of a transfer date.
4. Completion of the contract, including getting keys, transfer of funds, handling of any other payments (e.g. stamp duty in the UK) and registration of new ownership with the land registry.

You can ask friends, family or colleagues for a recommendation or you can refer to relevant websites in your country or region for a list of lawyers, e.g. www.lawyers.com in the US, solicitors.lawsociety.org.uk in the UK, www.findlaw.com.au in Australia and www.propertylawyers.org.nz in New Zealand.

The New Zealand Law Society has an excellent document on buying and selling a property. I would strongly recommend that you read it. You can find more details at https://www.lawsociety.org.nz/news-and-communications/guides-to-the-law/buying-and-selling-a-property

MAKING AN OFFER

If you like a property and are ready to move forward, then the next step is to make an offer on it (assuming it is not being sold via auction) through a Property Sale and Purchase Agreement.

Consider the asking price versus what you are willing to pay and make a sensible offer so that you leave room for negotiation. If the market is a buyers' market, you can make a very aggressive offer, given that you have the upper hand. If one offer does not go through another eventually will. However, if it is a sellers' market, you need to be very careful about the offer you make. Make sure your offer is serious enough to be considered, but also that you leave some room for negotiation.

It is also important to get a feel for what the seller is looking for, so feel free to fish for information and ask directly. You will be amazed how often people will let you know what they are looking for hence saving a lot of guesswork and negotiation time.

EXECUTING AND COMPLETING THE TRANSACTION

Once you have reached agreement with the vendor on the property price and other conditions, both parties sign the sales and purchase agreement. This can be done directly between the parties or via their respective lawyers.

The agreement will also stipulate if it is conditional (e.g. upon finance) and the date at which it would become unconditional. If any of the conditions are not met (e.g. you do not succeed in getting finance from the property) then you can annul the agreement by notifying the vendor accordingly. However, if all conditions are met and you are happy to proceed, you then accept the agreement as unconditional by notifying the vendor (ideally through your lawyer).

Your lawyer then handles the transaction from there on, ensuring that all necessary documentation is generated, and any bank conditions are met. They then proceed with the finalisation of the transaction and the money exchange.

Lastly, they arrange for you to receive the keys to your new home!

SECTION C - HOW TO MOVE FORWARD AND THRIVE

We keep moving forward, opening new doors and doing new things, because we're curious and curiosity keeps leading us down new paths.

-Walt Disney Company

CHAPTER 9: FINDING TENANTS AND MANAGING YOUR PROPERTY

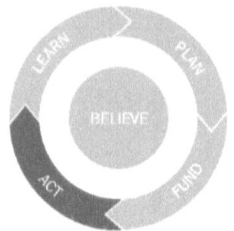

If you plan to rent out your property as an investment, then you need to be certain that you do this in a very professional manner rather than treating it as a little side activity.

In New Zealand, the www.tenancy.govt.nz website has great information on this topic (including various templates such as tenancy agreements) and has been a key source of information provided in this chapter. Similar websites in other countries are as below:

- US: www.landlordassociation.org
- UK: Residential Landlords Association (www.rla.org.uk)
- Australia: Property Owners Association of Australia (www.poaa.asn.au)

When I purchased my first and second properties I decided to rent and manage them myself, as I was keen to save property management fees. It all seemed to work out fine in the beginning, but I eventually found that I was investing a lot of time actively managing the tenants and chasing rents. One of the tenants was amazing and I never had any issue but the second one was a tenant from hell. Thankfully one of my work colleagues introduced me to his property manager who agreed to take on our properties. She worked for one of the big professional property managers at the time.

She managed the properties in an excellent manner but a year or so later she decided to become an independent property manager. She proposed to us to keep our portfolio with the existing company, as she did not have sufficient bandwidth. I was not totally happy about the idea, but I thought that, as we were in the hands of a reputable large player, we would be fine. I was totally wrong about that. Suddenly our tenants were turning over far more often, our rents were in arrears, maintenance costs started going through the roof and our relationship with this company dwindled.

I then decided to approach the original property manager and she kindly agreed to take on our portfolio. We have now been with her for almost 15 years!

TYPES OF TENANCIES

A tenancy is an agreement between a landlord and tenant. Tenancies will either tend to be short-term or long-term and in some cases, they will be of a shared-type.

According to www.gov.uk, a tenancy *"lets you live in a property as long as you pay rent and follow the rules. It also sets out the legal terms and conditions of your tenancy. It can be written down or oral (i.e. a spoken agreement).*

A tenancy can either be:

- *fixed-term (running for a set period of time).*
- *periodic (running on a week-by-week or month-by-month basis)".*

The key types of tenancies in the UK are:

1. **Assured Short-hold Tenancies (ASTs):** Most tenancies are automatically of this type and have certain criteria such as the property rental being private and the landlord not living in the property.
2. **Excluded Tenancies or Licenses:** Applies where the tenant shares part of the lodging with the landlord. The tenant has less protection from eviction compared to other tenancies.
3. **Assured Tenancies:** This type of tenancy has increased protection from eviction.
4. **Regulated Tenancies:** This type of tenancy has increased protection from eviction and the tenant can apply for 'fair rent', which is the legal maximum value determined by a rent officer from the Valuation Office Agency (VOA).

In New Zealand, the tenancy.govt.nz website describes the key types of tenancies as below:

1. **Periodic Tenancies:** *"A periodic tenancy is one that continues until either the tenant or the landlord gives written notice to end it."*

2. **Fixed-Term Tenancies:** *"A fixed-term tenancy only lasts for a set amount of time – for example, one year. The amount of time must be written on the tenancy agreement. If the fixed-term is for longer than 90 days, the tenancy automatically becomes a periodic tenancy when the fixed term expires (unless the landlord or the tenant gives notice to say they don't want the tenancy to continue or they agree on something else).*

   The landlord or tenant can't give notice to end a fixed-term tenancy early, so they both need to be very sure they want a fixed-term before they sign the tenancy agreement."

3. **Boarding Houses:** *"In a boarding house, a tenant rents a room, rather than the whole house. They share facilities such*

as the kitchen and bathroom with the other tenants. A boarding house is occupied, or intended to be occupied, by at least six tenants at any time."

You can make much higher returns with boarding houses, particularly close to schools, universities and other institutions; however, they require a lot more hands-on management and your wear and tear costs can also be higher.

The types of tenancies in Australia and the US are along the lines of those in New Zealand (i.e. Periodic and Fixed Term); however, the specific tenancy rules can vary by state.

FINDING TENANTS

There are many different ways in which you can find tenants for your property/properties:

1. Advertise on relevant online platforms in your country (e.g. on Zillow.com, Zoopla.co.uk, myproperty.com.au or Trademe.com).
2. Advertise in printed media (e.g. the NZ Herald or Sydney Morning Herald).
3. Advertise through property agents who have their own websites and marketing material.
4. Use your own network (physically or via social media) to spread the word.
5. Put a physical 'For Rent' sign on the property.

When you advertise your property, you need to ensure that you market it like a professional so that you get a good rental return from a reliable tenant as quick as possible. Below are some key tips on how to market your property:

1. Come up with a short but clear description of the property, with focus on key features of the property (e.g. location, number of rooms, etc.) and what makes it attractive (e.g. having 2 bathrooms, a large garden, being in a safe complex, etc.).
2. Take good photos (ideally get a professional to do this). If possible take photos with the place furnished so that potential tenants see it as a home rather than just a house.
3. Take short videos if possible to upload on the rental website.

Once you get any interested parties you need to go through the following steps:

1. Ask for some basic pre-application information to help you screen out those who do not fit your criteria (e.g. too large a family for the size of the property, lack of reliable income, etc.). Ensure that you are not breaking any rules in terms of the questions you are asking; e.g., in New Zealand, the www.tenancy.govt.nz website clearly states the questions you are allowed to ask.
2. Interview the potential tenants so you have a chance to ask them further questions and they have a chance to ask you any questions they may have.
3. Ask for references and check them.
4. Run a credit check to make sure your potential tenants have a good credit history. There are different agencies you can use for this, e.g. Lettingref.com in the UK and Trans Union – Smart Move (www.mysmartmove.com) in the US.

SETTING UP THE TENANCY AGREEMENT

Once you have selected your tenant and agreed on the appropriate type of tenancy, you will need to set up a tenancy agreement. If you find the tenant through a property manager, they will manage all this for you and you will only have to worry about signing the agreement. You can even avoid this if you give full rights to the property manager to represent you.

According to www.gov.uk, (and the same general principles would apply in most countries) the following items should be included in the agreement.

- The names of the parties involved.
- The rental price and the method of payment.
- Rental review.
- The deposit amount and method of protection.
- Any details around situations in which the deposit may be withheld.
- The property address, as well as the start and end date of the tenancy.
- Any other specific tenant or landlord obligations.
- Clarification of any bills the tenant will cover
- It can also include information on:
    - Any conditions around early termination of the tenancy.
    - Clarity around who pays for minor repairs.
    - Permission to sublet or have lodgers.

You can find the appropriate tenancy agreement templates on the relevant tenancy websites for your country. Some examples are as below:

- US: LawDepot (www.lawdepot.com)
- UK: www.gov.uk (they refer to the template as a 'model agreement')
- NZ: www.tenancy.govt.nz
- Queensland, Australia: www.rta.qld.gov.au

MANAGING YOUR PROPERTY

In my view it is best to let a professional manage your property. You may think you will save money by self-managing, but unless you are a gifted and natural property manager, you are better off handing the task over to someone who does management for a living and knows what they are doing. A good property manager will not only handle the day-to-day management of your property but will look after your investment.

Property management involves the following activities:

1. Finding tenants.
2. Setting up the tenancy agreements.
3. Regularly inspecting the properties.
4. Attending to any maintenance issues.
5. Collecting rent.
6. Following up on any rental arrears and following standard legal processes for this.
7. Managing end of tenancies.
8. Managing any tenant evictions.
9. Keeping you informed of any issues and getting your approval for any major expenses prior to these being incurred.

SELECTING YOUR PROPERTY MANAGER

As highlighted in my own story earlier in this chapter, the property manager you choose makes a big difference on the performance of your investment. A good property manager will ensure that you get fair market rent, high occupancy, that your property is well looked after and maintained, and any tenancy issues are swiftly resolved.

Before selecting a property manager, below are some questions you should ask them:

1. How many properties do you manage?
2. How many staff members do you have?
3. Do you have capacity to take on your property?
4. Which areas do you operate in?
5. What sort of experience do you have with tenancy tribunals?
6. How often do you pay out rental collections?
7. What sort of reports do you provide? (E.g. monthly statement, financial year statement, etc.) — also ask to see example reports.
8. How long does it typically take you to rent out a property?
9. What sort of vacancy rates do you currently have on your portfolio of properties?
10. How do you inspect and maintain the properties you manage? etc.

The intention of the above, or similar questions, is for you to determine if the property manager has the right experience, qualifications and tools, and is the right person to work with you.

You will also need to set up an agreement with your property manager. If they are a professional, they will supply the agreement but be sure to seek legal advice before signing any agreement in case you are not familiar with such agreements.

MAINTAINING YOUR PROPERTY

It is crucial that you properly maintain your property, not only because you want it to be in good condition for your tenants (therefore ensuring good rental returns), but also to extend the life of your property and avoid unforeseen large expenses (e.g. regular cleaning of the spouting increases its lifespan).

REVIEWING YOUR RENTS

On average, rents will go up with inflation, and in some cases where demand is very high, the rental growth will exceed inflation, as has been the case in major cities such as Auckland and Sydney in recent years. If you have multi-year tenancy agreements, you'll need to include a rental increase clause based on Consumer Price Inflation (CPI). If you have a periodic tenancy agreement, you must keep an eye on market rents and increase your rents appropriately. There is a process to follow when increasing rents, so this should be done by the book. Refer to the relevant tenancy website in your country or state.

CHAPTER 10: ADDING VALUE TO YOUR PROPERTY

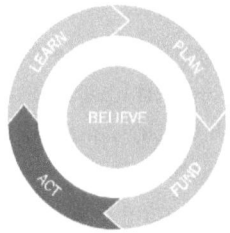

WHY ADD VALUE

It is a no brainer to add further value to your property when it is practical and makes financial sense. If this is done properly it can:

- Improve the property and enhance your chances of getting better rental returns.
- Increase the property value and your equity, which can enable you to grow your portfolio. The general view is that if the value addition is done properly, the project cost will be about 25%, with the other 75% going back into the property through increased value.
- Increase the life of your asset, e.g. if you give the property a good exterior paint, resolve any structural issues, replace old windows, etc., you could give your old property a new lease of life.
- Reduce maintenance and energy costs, e.g. if you replace your old windows with modern, double-glazed ones and add a heat pump, you would reduce your energy bills and also reduce dampness in the property, which reduces maintenance costs.

BASIC WAYS TO ADD VALUE TO YOUR PROPERTY

There are some very cost effective and quick ways to add value to your property, as listed below:

1. **Improve your front door** — you will be amazed at how adding an attractive front door can improve the look of your house in terms of its desirability and value. If you have an old, boring door, do some research and find a way to replace it with a classier and more interesting one!
2. **Keep the external part of the house clear and give it a fresh coat of paint** — this will increase the attractiveness of the house. Even though we say that a book should not be judged by its cover, we all know that we do it regardless!
3. **Upgrade the kitchen** — many people consider the kitchen to be the heart of the home. To this end, sensibly upgrading your kitchen without going overboard can add value to your home. You can reportedly recoup up to 120% of your cost through an appropriate kitchen upgrade. In many cases, simply repainting the kitchen, adding splashbacks behind the sink and oven, and upgrading to new, energy efficient appliances can substantially improve the kitchen. This can also make your home more attractive to potential buyers in the future.
4. **Upgrade the bathroom** — an upgraded bathroom can really lift the look and comfort of a home. The first step is to be certain that the bathroom is functional, e.g. the wiring and plumbing are safe and working effectively. Nothing is worse than seeing hanging wires, bad lighting and leaky pipes or taps in a bathroom. The next step is to assess if any improvements can be made without making layout changes, e.g. upgrading bathroom cabinets, replacing tiles, upgrading the sink and shower, etc. Lastly, consider any layout changes if absolutely necessary, as they will come at a much higher cost.
5. **Change door handles** — old door handles can make a house look old-fashioned. They do not cost a lot and it is amazing

how modern, attractive door handles can lift the look of the house. *My property in London had old roundish and golden door handles. They not only looked old-fashioned but also old and used. We replaced these with sturdy and modern handles and it was amazing how this small improvement completely changed the look of the interior!*

6. **Tidy up the garden** — a tidy garden will not only make your property look better but will also increase the perceived/usable size of your garden.

7. **Change your curtains** — old or inappropriate curtains could make your entire property look old and unattractive and reduce its perceived value. New and tasteful curtains can really improve the look of your home.

8. **Change your carpet or flooring** — an old carpet or flooring can make your property look worn-out. A new carpet or floor with a fresh coat of paint could entirely change the look and feel of your property.

9. **Pave the front section of the house rather than having a garden** — this gives more parking space (particularly in parking constrained areas) and impacts the value of the property.

10. **Swap out old windows with double-glazed ones** — this makes the home more energy efficient and adds value to it.

11. **Add mirrors in strategic areas to enhance spaciousness** — everyone wants a sense of more space in their home. More sense of space equals willingness to pay more.

12. **Add storage space — particularly higher up** — this tends to be wasted space (e.g. in kitchens, bedrooms and hallways). In space-constrained cities, e.g. London and Paris, storage space is priceless. If you can smartly add storage space, it will make your property far more attractive both from a rental and a sales perspective.

13. **Add central heating to the house** — people want to live comfortably and at the same time would like to know that

their energy bills are under control. Central heating substantially improves the living comfort — it is warm throughout the house and you do not get the sense of dampness that comes with the alternative — and at the same time, it is far more cost effective than having electric or other types of heaters in different parts of the house. The increase in value to your property could be as much as double your investment amount.

14. **Have larger doors that lead to the garden and ideally make these glass doors** — this will further add a sense of space to your house and will also improve your experience living in the house.

15. **Add decking to appropriate areas** — this, again, makes better use of the land around your house and improves your living experience. It touches the emotions of the people, e.g. with good decking, someone could visualise barbeques or parties and become attached to the property.

16. **Add a decent garden shed** — this further provides more storage space and, as stated earlier, in space-constrained places additional storage space is priceless.

It would also be well worth it to get professional advice from an estate agent, builder or interior designer on how you can cost effectively improve your property.

The advantage of doing any property improvement work is that you do not have to do it all at the same time. You can do it gradually and take baby steps as necessary if you do not have sufficient funds or time.

MORE ADVANCED WAYS OF ADDING VALUE TO YOUR PROPERTY

There are ways to add even more value, but these cost a bit more and can take some time and patience to do:

1. **Add a room** — in general, the more rooms you have in your house, the higher the price and rent, even if the total floor area does not change!
2. **Knock down walls to create more open space (e.g. between the living room and kitchen)** — people want a sense of space in their house and will always be willing to pay more for it.
3. **Add a toilet / bathroom** — no one likes to wait to go to the bathroom or have a shower. Additionally, we all love an ensuite room. So adding an extra toilet/bathroom will generally always add value.
4. **Convert your garage to a granny flat** — a granny flat can be independently let so the flat not only increases the value of the property but also substantially increases rental returns.
5. **Build a granny flat if you have spare land** — as above.
6. **Build a conservatory if you do not have sufficient land for a granny flat** — a conservatory can be used as an office, storage area or living space. It will add value to your property.
7. **Subdivide the land and build another house / flat** — subdividing your land and being able to sell it separately will give you returns well over and above what you will invest. In essence you have taken something that was one and now you have two. Of course, this comes at a cost, including the building of a new property on the subdivided land, but the overall returns should far surpass the investment, if it is done properly
8. **Rebuild from scratch** — if you have a very old house or have sufficient land to build a larger property (e.g. with multiple

flats) then it is well worth flattening the current building and starting from scratch to optimise land use.

As highlighted earlier, the area where I grew up in Nairobi used to have large villas. However, due to increased population density and high demand for housing, that whole area has changed so much that I cannot recognise it today. All the lovely villas have been replaced by high-rise flats. But clearly these have given much higher returns to their owners than what the old villas did.

I have personally added value to my properties using most of the examples above. I have also done this gradually over the past few years. I never let my property portfolio sit still — I am always looking for ways to increase value, increase returns and reduce costs! I am sure the time will soon come for me to also use point 8 above!

As an example, one of my properties was on about 1,000sqm of land. It was a 3-bed property with a double garage. In the early days, council rules did not allow for the land to be subdivided due to its shape and other constraints. But subsequent planning changes enabled me to fully subdivide and put up a brand new 3-bed and 2-bathroom property. I also converted the garage to a two-bedroom granny flat. This has not only more than doubled the value of my property, albeit with a decent amount of investment, but has substantially increased the rental returns of my property.

I converted the garage of one of my two-bed units to a rumpus room with an additional bathroom. This has probably increased the value of the property by over $50,000, and again, given the ability to get at least $50 extra rent per week. It is also highly beneficial for the tenant, as they can have a larger family live more comfortably in the unit, or they could have a flatmate so as *to get some additional income — this could, in turn, allow them to start saving for their own property! A true win-win situation!*

A close friend in London bought a 1-bed flat in the Westbourne area (very close to Notting Hill). You would be amazed what a 1-bed flat in that area costs. When I first saw it, I absolutely loved it (due to its location and style as well as its charming balcony) but it seemed a bit small. The bedroom in particular felt tight and his bed took up a decent amount of space. Within a few months he had remodelled the kitchen/lounge area and suddenly the flat looked and felt much more spacious. That £5,000 investment probably added well over £20,000 value. I then visited his flat some months later and lo and behold the whole place had changed again. I literally thought that I was in a new home. He had somehow once managed to create a lot more space in the lounge by using a smart kitchen design and he had remodelled the bedroom. It no longer looked small, and his new bed fitted perfectly with lots of space left. He also used mirrors in strategic spots to further give a feeling of spaciousness.

I hope that with the examples above you can see that this is not all theory. You *can* change your living space and, in the process, add substantial value to your house by making a few smart improvements.

HOW TO ADD VALUE IN A COST-EFFECTIVE MANNER

Improving your property will definitely cost some money but you can do this in a cost-effective way:

- Do your homework: Have a good understanding of what work is needed.

- Do it yourself: If you are a handy kind of person, or are willing to learn to do handy work, you will save substantial money by doing any improvements yourself.

  My wife and I retiled a big portion of our bathroom in London without any prior experience. We bought the necessary tools and got a few tips from friends and online sources. We probably saved over £2,000 by doing the work ourselves.

- Get friends or family to help you do the work. Even if you pay them, it would be far more cost effective than getting a builder you do not know.
- Get multiple quotes so that you can choose the most cost-effective option.
- Use tradesman hiring websites like myjobquote.co.uk. Such websites enable you to advertise your renovation job and multiple tradesmen then pitch for the work. You can then select the person or company you see most fit for the job based on their pitch and their ratings.

  I recently used the myjobquote.co.uk website site to select tradesmen to renovate my entire property in London and I am certain that I saved thousands of pounds by using this website.

- Do the work in a staged manner so you can manage the costs.
- Focus first on what creates most value. The good old 80-20 rule applies in everything. You will often find that you can add 80% value by making only 20% changes, provided you choose those changes wisely.

In general, my view is that one should prioritise the living space, kitchen and external parts of the house, as these are the parts that are most visible and where people spend most of their time.

CHAPTER 11: GROWING YOUR PORTFOLIO

KNOW WHAT YOU WANT AND WHEN YOU WANT IT

If you get into a car and start randomly driving without knowing where you want to go, how long will you drive, and what direction will you take? Where will you get to? You may get very lucky and end up somewhere nice, but what is the likelihood of that? You may already have heard of the expression "The harder I work, the luckier I get" — I like to think of it as "the *smarter* I work, the luckier I get". To work smart, you need to have a clear set of objectives and a plan to achieve them.

Let us get more specific in terms of building your property portfolio. You can set your objectives in different ways, but below are some examples:

- I want to own 10 properties within the next 20 years
- I want to have a property portfolio worth $5 million in the next 5 years
- I want a beautiful, 5-bed property by the sea and an investment property that gives me passive income of $20,000 per year, etc.

Once you have a clear idea of what you want, you need to make it a part of you. Think of it at least twice a day and visualise that you have already achieved your desires (see Chapter 16 for more information on this).

You may be thinking that all this sounds airy fairy, but this is what numerous successful people (even billionaires) have done to achieve their desires.

When I bought my first property, I barely squeezed out enough cash to buy a simple 2-bed unit. But because I had surrounded myself with like-minded people who wanted to be successful and I was reading books (like this one) that were expanding my mind and belief in myself, something changed in me. At that stage I had a simple objective — buy at least one property every 2 years. In the 15 years that have passed since then, I have surpassed my initial goal. However, at that stage, despite not having a clue how exactly I was going to be able to buy a property every 2 years, I simply knew that I was going to do it.

Every single time I have set out a clear objective and somehow deeply believed that I will achieve it, I have managed to achieve it. When I was young and growing up in Kenya, I somehow always knew that I would go study and live overseas, even though my family at that stage did not have enough money to fund me. At that time, I did not even dare to dream that I would end up in one of the top business schools in the world, but in my late 20s, that desire started burning in me and I somehow just knew that I would do an MBA at a top business school. I even forgot about it for a while but through sheer serendipity, I was talking to a friend who said that he was thinking of doing an MBA. For some reason, that night I started doing some research and one thing led to another and within 2 years I was studying at London Business School.

As I started my MBA, a whole new world opened and I was surrounded by amazing minds and some extremely wealthy people. Not only did I learn a lot about the business world and what ticks it, along with the technical skills required for it, but I made great friends and totally changed my mindset. My simple motto is: "Believe, visualise, work smart and achieve". Of course, I still have a lot more to do and achieve in life, but I feel assured that I somehow will.

So I invite you to be bold with your desire, write it down and even shout it out loud — over and over. Deeply believe that you will achieve your goal and I can assure you nothing will stop you from achieving it!

HAVE A PLAN

Once you know what you want, you need to come up with a high-level plan on how to achieve it. Let us take an example in which you want to own 5 properties in 20 years. If we do simple math on this, then you need to buy an average of 1 property every 4 years. You can then break that down even further by putting down the value of the properties you plan to purchase and what finances you will need to purchase these.

EXECUTE YOUR PLAN AND RE-PLAN AS NECESSARY

Regularly look at your plan (ideally every single day) and keep yourself on track and take the actions you are supposed to take.

If your intention is to buy a property every 4 years, you need to save accordingly and look at potential new acquisitions. You need to be fully abreast of the market and if you feel that you will not be able to buy in your own city or country, then look beyond that. But be certain that you are keeping to your plan. You will be amazed to find that doors you did not even imagine existed will open. Money will come from sources you least expected and buying opportunities will also come.

The reason for this is simple. You will have tuned your frequency to property acquisition mode and you will therefore attract everything on that frequency including funding and buying opportunities. However, if you are on the frequency of not believing that you can grow your portfolio and not taking action to grow your portfolio then that is the frequency you will be on and that is what you will attract.

Let us put this theory into action. When was the last time you saw a lime green car? I am sure that most of you will not have seen one, either ever, or for a very long time. Now try to focus on seeing a lime green car in the coming days and see if you see at least one if not more. If you are on the frequency of seeing a lime green car then I can assure you that you will see one very soon — physically, online or some other way!

The closer you stay to the property market in your chosen location(s), the more you will be aware of the market dynamics and the more aware you will be of opportunities. Sometimes opportunities can come in the least expected ways. Let us say you did your absolute best to save for a new property, but you simply could not make enough equity. Perhaps you will come across a piece of land you could buy, or perhaps you will find that you could add another flat to an existing property you own, or perhaps you could go into partnership with someone. **Seek and you shall find!**

Keep the growth ticking along, and within a few years and you will look back in amazement at how your portfolio has grown.

I have a very simple analogy for this. If you know where you want to go, and you get into a car and drive towards that destination, as each second passes by you get closer and closer to your destination. After moving to Botswana, I got into mountain biking and eventually signed up for a race called the Kalahari Challenge. It is a gruelling 250km race over three days with very rocky, hilly and sandy terrain. I would not have even dreamt of doing this race before, but after training with some friends, I just got into the training rhythm. We were once riding with some other people I had never met and got along with one of the riders in particular. He gave me a simple tip — keep pedalling — when you are feeling strong, pedal — when you are weak, keep pedalling — when you are extremely tired — keep pedalling. And during the competition, (despite not having had too much time to train) that is what I did and I managed to finish the race in a decent time that I was happy with.

However hard it feels to buy that next property, keep doing the work, keep finding ways to get money, keep looking for properties to buy, keep looking for ways to add value to what you have, **keep moving, do not stop! Do not stop! There will be good times and there will be tough times — but do not stop!**

So that this is all not just theory and mumbo jumbo, let us work through a practical example that an average income earner might go through.

- 3-bed property purchased in 2012 for $500,000 with 20% equity
- Annual mortgage repayments (assuming 20-year loan at 5% interest with capital repayments) = $32,100 (monthly = $2,675)
- Current value of property = $805,300 (assuming 10% value increase p.a. per recent growth in New Zealand)
- Current Debt = $333,000
- Current Equity = $805,300 - $333,000 = $472,100
- Current Leverage (Debt) = $333,000 / $805,300 = 41%

You then decide to purchase a 2-bed unit at $500,000 and you have managed to save $50,000 in the past 5 years. Let us examine what the numbers would look like and how you would be able to afford this.

	Current Property	New Property	Portfolio
Value	805,300	500,000	1,305,300
Debt	333,000	450,000	783,000
Equity	472,300	50,000	522,300
Debt%	41.4%	90.0%	60.0%
Equity%	58.6%	10.0%	40.0%
Mortgage (interest only)	32,100	22,500	54,600
Net Rent (after exp)*	0	20,000	20,000
Net Outflow	32,100	2,500	34,600
Increased Outflow			2,500

*Assume $480 rent per week (5% gross yield) and about 20% expenses

You would therefore end up with a 60% overall debt ratio (which even with today's strict conditions for investors would be acceptable to the banks and regulator) and you would only need to pay about $200 extra per month (after catering for the net rent received after all expenses), which would be fairly affordable for a family on an average income. Within a few years, once rents have gone and/or if you reduce your mortgage, you would end up with positive rather than negative cash flow.

Strictly speaking, it is better to have a neutral or positive cash flow property. Therefore, in the above example, you should endeavour to reduce your mortgage as quickly as possible so that you could turn it into a positive cash flow investment.

MAXIMISE YOUR RETURNS

I will let you in on a little secret on how top management consultants and strategists go about solving very complex problems. It is through using frameworks to break down and simplify the problem. When I did my MBA and prepared for job interviews, I had to do numerous rounds of what was called 'crack a case'. In essence you are given a business situation and you have to find a solution to it. And in order to find the solution, you need to use a sensible framework.

The reason I am talking about all this at this point of the book is because one of the simplest frameworks used and applicable in numerous situations is the 'Profitability' framework.

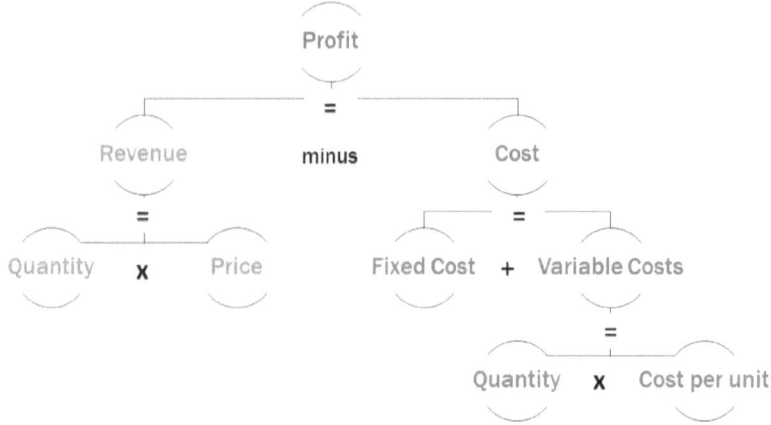

The above picture shows the very simple profitability framework, but you will be amazed at how many insights this can give you. Let us talk through it from a property investment perspective. If you want to maximise your returns from your property portfolio then you need to:

1. Maximise revenue
2. Minimise cost

MAXIMISING REVENUE

To maximise revenue, the levers you have are to increase:

1. **Quantity:** So from a property perspective that would mean:

a. Having more properties; or
b. More streams of revenue from a given property, e.g.
    i. if you are letting out the property on a room-by-room basis, you could increase the number of rooms
    ii. If you are letting out your property on a daily basis through a channel such as Airbnb, you would need to increase the number of days that the property is rented

2. **Price:** From a property perspective that would mean increasing your rent.

Whenever I review this framework for my own properties, it is a good reminder for me to review my rents and check to see that they reflect any recent market rental increases. And in New Zealand this has happened a number of times in recent years due to high rental demand.

MINIMISING COST

In order to minimise your property costs, below are some of the relevant levers. The idea is not just to reduce costs without focusing on the quality of work, or reliability of the people you will deal with (e.g. property managers) — the focus should be on getting the best value for money (i.e. where cost is minimised but without compromising quality).

Fixed Costs:

Unless you are a professional and larger property investor, you are unlikely to have fixed costs such as office rental, staff costs, etc. However, if you *do* have any such costs, you should assess if there are any areas where these costs could be reduced (e.g.

negotiating a lower rent for your office, finding ways to reduce staffing costs, e.g. through outsourcing or automation, etc.).

Variable Costs:

From a property investment perspective, the biggest costs will tend to be variable, based on the number of properties you have. A variable cost is that which increases with the quantity of product (number of properties in this case).

1. **Interest rates:** Mortgage interest is one of the highest costs when you have a property portfolio and you use debt to finance a part of it.

   I have personally managed to save thousands of dollars by constantly looking at this to be sure that that I am getting the best deal. Oftentimes I have broken my fixed-term mortgage and even paid a fee for it, but it has been worth doing, as overall it has saved me substantial interest costs.

2. **Maintenance costs:** Shop around and make sure you are getting a good deal. It is amazing how the cost of a simple job such as tiling can be reduced by shopping around and getting multiple quotes. If you find a good, reliable handyman, establish a good relationship with him/her and set up an agreement for ongoing work if possible.

3. **Property management fees:** In New Zealand, for example, property management fees can vary substantially, starting at 8% and going up to over 12%. So you might want to either look for the most cost-effective property manager, or negotiate a reduction in the fees of your existing property manager if the fee you are paying is too high. In the UK, these fees are even higher, so it becomes even more important to try and find a cost effective, but quality, property manager.

4. **Insurance costs:** You will have different types of insurance costs: building insurance, contents insurance, rental insurance, etc. Insurance costs can also vary a lot so it is very important to search for a reputable, but affordable, company. That said, when it comes to insurance, it is always better to go for quality over price.

    We were able to reduce the insurance cost of one of our properties by 20% recently simply by looking around and getting a quote from another reputable insurance company.

5. **Other miscellaneous costs:** There will be other costs, such as accountant fees, legal fees, etc. Do your homework so that you don't end up overpaying.

    I recently needed to change the ownership structure of my portfolio, and by looking around, I saved 50% legal cost without impacting the quality of the work or the outcome.

I am going to go off-piste here for a short while to give a broader view of the consultant frameworks that can come in very handy with any of your business initiatives, whether relating to real estate or not. It is incredible how these frameworks can help you get to the crux of the problem and analyse the situation optimally. For example, if you wanted to start a new business, below is the 3-Cs framework you could use to assess your ability to succeed in that business:

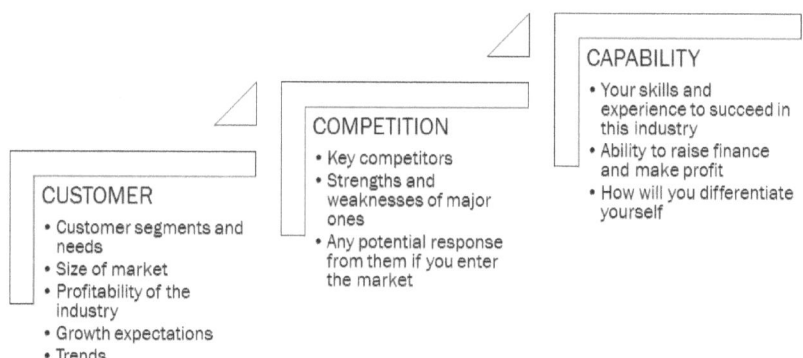

There are many books on this subject, and plenty of rich material online. I would highly encourage you to look into this further. An example of a good book on this is *Key Management Models, 3rd Edition: The 75+ Models Every Manager Needs to Know (3rd Edition)* by Marcel Van Assen, Gerben Van den Berg and Paul Pietersma.

BE HAPPY AND CELEBRATE YOUR ACHIEVEMENTS

One thing to be careful of is not to tie your happiness with your achievements. Happiness is a way of being and it comes from the inside rather than the outside.

I used to have a completely different view in the past and used to think that happiness is moments that you steal from life. But after reading some interesting, thought-provoking books on this subject such as *The Power of Now* by Elkhart Tolle, I completely changed my mind. Now I think that sadness consists of the moments you steal from life.

The happier you are, and the more satisfied you are with life, the calmer and more mindful you will be and that will place you in a much better position to spot opportunities and grow your wealth. So be happy with what you already have and celebrate in true style when you achieve more. Do not forget to be thankful to the universe for helping you on the way. Otherwise you will continue to chase happiness thinking that you will be happy when you just get that next big property or anything else. And you may end up looking back at your life and wondering that, despite all you managed to amass, did you actually enjoy your life and fill it with moments of happiness?

HAVE A CLEAR VIEW OF YOUR CASHFLOW AND FINANCES AT A PORTFOLIO LEVEL

It much easier to value a single property and manage cash flow; however, once you have two or more properties you need to have a clear view of your finances at a portfolio level. Below is a simple example in Excel on how you could do that:

	PROPERTIES			
	1	2	3	TOTAL
Purchase Price	400,000	300,000	500,000	1,200,000
Fees & Stamp Duty (if a	8,000	6,000	10,000	24,000
Total Purchase Price	408,000	306,000	510,000	1,224,000
Rent p.m.	1,600	1,250	2,000	4,850
Est. Vacancy Rate	3%	3%	3%	
Total Income p.a.	18,624	14,550	23,280	56,454 = Rent x 12 x (1 - Vacancy Rate)
PM Fees p.a.	1,920	1,500	2,400	5,820 = E.g. approx 10% of Annual Rent
Insurance / Rates p.a.	800	600	1,000	2,400 = E.g. approx 0.2% of Purchase Price
Maintenance p.a.	1,200	900	1,500	3,600 = E.g. approx 0.3% of Purchase Price
Interest Rate	4.0%	5.0%	5.0%	
Interest Amount p.a.	9,600	10,500	17,500	37,600 = Interest Rate x Mortgage Balance
Net Income	5,104	1,050	880	7,034 = Total Income - All Expenses
Tax (30% marginal rate)	1,531	315	264	2,110
Net Income after Tax	3,573	735	616	4,924
Gross Yield on Purchase	4.7%	4.9%	4.7%	
Net Yield on Purchase	1.3%	0.3%	0.2%	
Market Yield	4%	5%	3%	
Est. Property Value	480,000	300,000	800,000	1,580,000 = Annual Rent / Market Yield
Debt	240,000	210,000	350,000	800,000 = Current Mortgage Balance
Net Equity	240,000	90,000	450,000	780,000 = Property Value - Debt

p.m. = Per Month

p.a. = Per Annum

The above example is simplified to give an appreciation of the concept of understanding and tracking your finances at a portfolio level. It assumes an interest-only loan and a marginal tax rate of 30%. If you have loan with capital repayments, then you would need to include the loan repayments in order to compute your net cash flow. Additionally, your actual tax would depend on other factors such as an impending tax credits, any other expenses not reflected above, etc.

CHAPTER 12: YOUR EXIT STRATEGY AND SELLING YOUR PROPERTY

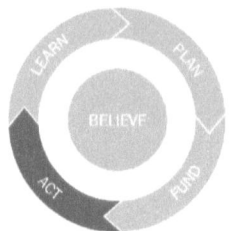

YOUR OVERALL EXIT STRATEGY

With any business or investment, one needs an exit strategy. Whether you have a single property or a massive portfolio you need to think about an eventual exit.

For example, your exit strategy may be to:

- Sell the property and downsize when you reach retirement
- Keep the property through your retirement and have your family inherit it
- Keep the full portfolio and fully or partly live off the cash flow
- Sell part of the portfolio to make the rest of the portfolio debt-free so you can fully or partly live off the rents
- Sell the full portfolio and put the returns into a low-risk investment and live off the returns
- Sell a property and upgrade once you have sufficient funds or equity in the existing property, etc.

Once you have a clear exit strategy, you can grow and manage your assets so that what you do with the assets is aligned with your eventual exit strategy. Not having an exit strategy is like getting on a random train without knowing your final destination.

WHEN TO SELL YOUR PROPERTY

The overall timing of the sale of one or more of your properties should be tied to your exit strategy as discussed above. Once you decide to go ahead with the sale, you need to time that sale well. For example, if you sell during a down-cycle (recession) you will realise much lower returns than in an up-cycle. Clearly, if you are desperate for cash and need to sell, you will need to sell as quickly as possible, otherwise you should time the sale correctly so that you maximise your returns. Also, if you are planning to sell a given property and buy another in the same city/country then even if it is a down market, that should not be a problem; although you will get lower returns for your property, you will also be able to buy your new property at a lower value.

HOW TO SELL YOUR PROPERTY

PRIVATE SALE VERSUS USING AN AGENT

You can sell your property through an agent or privately. Selling privately would save you agent fees of 2% - 5%; however, be wary of the following risks/downsides:

1. You will need to spend a lot of your own time marketing and selling the property (e.g. you will need to arrange viewings and be on site for these).
2. You may not know the correct market values and because of that you would not realise the full potential value of your property. Even after considering the 2%-5% fee you may have paid, you may have still been better off by selling via an agent.
3. You may not market your property as well as your agent or reach as many people, which can cause the sale of the property to take longer.

You can reduce the agent's fee by going exclusive with a specific agent, as they tend to give a discount for an exclusive contract for a certain period of time.

AUCTION VS. SALE BY NEGOTIATION

Auctions are better in seller markets (i.e. where demand exceeds supply), as you can end up getting a higher than expected value for your property. However, in buyer markets (i.e. where supply exceeds demand), a sale by negotiation could give you better returns provided you are not in a rush.

MARKETING YOUR PROPERTY

Just like when you are renting your property (as highlighted in Chapter 9), there are many different ways in which you can make your property more visible to potential buyers:

1. Advertise on relevant online platforms (e.g. on Zoopla, Zillow or Trademe.com).
2. Advertise in printed media (e.g. the NZ Herald).
3. Advertise through property agents who have their own websites and marketing material.
4. Use your own network (physically or via social media) to spread the word.
5. Put a physical 'For Sale' sign on the property.

When you advertise your property, you need to market it like a professional to get the best value for your asset as quickly as possible. Below are some key tips on how to market your property:

1. Come up with a short but clear description of the property with a focus on the key features of the property (e.g. location, number of rooms, etc.) and what makes it attractive (e.g.

having 2 bathrooms, having a large garden, being in a safe complex, etc.).

2. Take good photos (ideally get a professional to do this). If possible, take photos with the place furnished so that potential tenants see it as a 'home' rather than just a 'house'.

3. Take short videos, if possible, to upload on the selling website.

LAWYER

Get a good solicitor (possibly the same one who helped you with the purchase) to help execute the property sale transaction.

As highlighted in the property buying section, you can ask friends, family or colleagues for a recommendation or you can refer to the relevant websites in your country (www.lawyers.com in the US, solicitors.lawsociety.org.uk in the UK, www.findlaw.com.au in Australia and www.propertylawyers.org.nz in New Zealand) for a list of property lawyers in your area.

The New Zealand Law Society has an excellent document on buying and selling a property. I would strongly recommend that you read it. The same principles apply in most countries; however, you could find the equivalent site for your country or region.

You can find more details at https://www.lawsociety.org.nz/news-and-communications/guides-to-the-law/buying-and-selling-a-property.

SALES AND PURCHASE AGREEMENT

When you get one or more offers, you will need to complete a Sales and Purchase Agreement. Make certain that you are happy with any conditions the potential buyer has specified. Seek advice from your lawyer if necessary, as the last thing you want to do is to sign a conditional agreement with a buyer who is not serious and has many options to back out of the transaction.

To reduce the risk of any buyer backing out of the transaction, try to get back-up agreements.

EXECUTING THE SALES TRANSACTION

Once the Sales and Purchase Agreement is unconditionally signed by the buyer, your lawyer will help manage the rest of the process. This will include:

1. Transfer of title
2. Handing over of keys
3. Repayment of any existing mortgage you may have on the property

CHAPTER 13: KEY PITFALLS AND HOW TO AVOID THESE

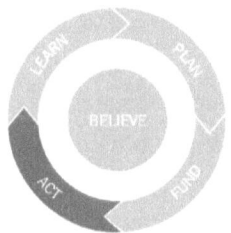

There are many pitfalls that one could fall into in the property world. Below are some of most prominent snares from my perspective. If you can avoid these, you can substantially reduce the risk of property purchase or investments.

1. NOT HAVING A STRATEGY AND/OR CLEAR OBJECTIVES

As noted earlier, not having a strategy and objectives is like getting on a random train, without knowing where you want to go or which route you will take. Knowing where you want to go is a good start but having one or more routes in mind before you start will make the whole journey far easier, quicker and more successful!

I have a simple philosophy — "If you know where you want to go, and you have a route in mind then with every second that passes by you get closer and closer to your destination. If you keep moving, then you are bound to get to your destination!" Clearly, life is not always that simple but if you always keep your objectives in mind (and there is no reason why objectives cannot change sometimes due to changing priorities and life situations), have a route and adjust it as necessary, and you keep moving forward, your likelihood of success is going to be much higher than someone who does not have a plan.

Some people can get very lucky in the property market regardless of what they buy if they time it right — particularly when the market is in an up-cycle and property prices are growing year after year. However, if you do not have a clear strategy and objectives, you could end up either losing money or not making as much money as you could have if you bought in a more astute manner.

Let us take a simple example: A couple has devised a strategy where they will buy an apartment to begin their journey on the property ladder. They will then save and build their incomes in order to afford a second home. They also wish to rent out their first home after they've moved. With that in mind, they determine how much they need to save per month and for how long. They also assess other avenues for getting their down payment, e.g. selling their car, borrowing from family, etc. They then accumulate their down payment through savings and the other means they have determined. They purchase a sensible apartment that suits their short-term personal needs and is also a decent rental investment in the long run. They then make a plan for further savings and also use equity in their existing apartment (assuming house prices grow) to fund the down payment of their new home in a few years' time.

Now take an example of another couple. This couple sort of wants a family home but does not have any plan on what they want or how to go about getting it. They would spend years trying to get on the property ladder, struggling to make sufficient money to cover the down payment, and even if they eventually manage, they may not see the same level of success as the couple who had a clear plan — if they are lucky they would end up with one property.

This example is not hypothetical at all. There are numerous people stuck in this situation. I know that I was in this category at one stage and perhaps you also fall in this group. Do you? If so, you have most of the answers in this book to help you change!

If you are an investor, then having a strategy is even more critical. You need to have a clear idea of whether you are chasing potential capital gains on a long-term basis, you want cash flow through rental income, or you want to make quick cash through flipping. You may even have a strategy that combines all these approaches in a balanced manner. If you do not think through your investments then, for example, you may end up with a property that leaves you very cash strapped, as you may have to cover mortgage payments due to insufficient rental income and you may even be forced to sell it.

2. OVERTHINKING AND NOT BUYING

I love Richard Branson's motto of *'screw it, just do it'*. Now neither Richard nor I are saying that one should make senseless moves and investments in life but the main message here is that it does no good to overthink things and let opportunities pass you by while other people grab onto them and grow. If you find an opportunity and it makes sense, e.g. if you have just enough money to buy a small unit that would be good enough for now rather than the home of your dreams, go for it! At least you will have your own home and an asset. Yes, you may compromise on a bit on space or some comforts, but you will be on the property ladder. If you are disciplined and continue to make savings and take advantage of any growth of value of your existing property, then in time you could either upgrade or buy an additional property.

3. AVOIDING CONFLICTS AND INVOLVEMENT OF LAWYERS

Conflicts between tenants and landlords can easily happen. If you are a landlord, firstly, confirm that you do everything by the book (i.e. follow the rule of law) and secondly, do your best to avoid unnecessary conflicts and the involvement of lawyers.

I privately rented out a UK property and for two years the tenancy went like a dream. But just a few months before the tenant was due to vacate the property, for some reason, he felt that he had been overpaying for it and demanded that I return some of the money. From my end he had been paying the market rent and if he had felt that it was too expensive then he had the choice to either negotiate at the outset or not rent the flat at all. So I refused and unfortunately the situation became very emotional and we started exchanging very unfriendly emails. I eventually decided to engage a lawyer, as I felt that the whole thing was spiralling out of control, particularly when the tenant threatened not to pay rent and vacate the property. A silly mistake I made was to lodge his deposit with the governing authority a few days late, and this put me in a very compromising position, as according to the UK rules, this prevented me from issuing a notice to forcefully remove the tenant — this is a very bizarre nuance of the UK tenancy rules, but I sadly found this too late!

Eventually I had to settle with the tenant and lost over £5,000 in lost rent and legal fees of over £3,000. If I had kept a cool mind and reached a settlement with the tenant right at the outset, I would have probably lost only £1,000 to £2,000. The moral of the story is:

- *If you are renting a property privately, be sure you follow the rules to the dot.*
- *If you have a disagreement with a tenant, avoid conflict and try to reach an agreement even if it means you lose some money.*
- *Only involve lawyers if you have absolutely no choice, as this is going to cost you an arm and a leg! Clearly, there are situations where there is no choice and the cost is well worth it. Lawyers, particularly good ones, are there for a very good reason.*

4. INVESTMENT IN NEW DEVELOPMENTS WITHOUT EXPERIENCE (E.G. APARTMENTS AND GATED ESTATES)

It is critical that you have either done a lot of research and homework or have experience in new developments before you buy a new apartment or home in a gated community off-the-plan. Not only do you face the general risk of new developments, but you are reliant on the whole development (or a big logical chunk of it) being completed before you will be able to take ownership of your property and either stay in it or rent it out. You will need to make capital payments during key phases of development and if you are borrowing money you will need to make interest payments before you have full ownership of your property. You really need to take this cost into consideration as it can have a big impact on your returns, particularly if there are major delays to the development.

I fell into this trap myself some time back. I somehow managed to make a mistake that I could have avoided.

I bought a property in Botswana while I was living there as an expatriate. I went ahead with the purchase, as the property market had been doing really well in the few years before my arrival there. Botswana is one of the most stable countries of Africa, with a decent GDP per capita and a good standard of living. It has some of the most profitable and largest diamond mines in the world. I, therefore, felt that it would be a very good place to invest.

The most sensible thing would have been to buy a house as soon as I arrived and then to live in it. This would have guaranteed rent on my investment, as my company was covering my rent. However, it took me time to decide to buy due to other priorities.

One of my local work colleagues told me about a development where she was going to buy a property. The developer had successfully completed two major gated estates in the previous ten years and had a decent reputation. The location of the development was good, and the price also seemed reasonable. I did my usual due diligence and financial assessments, and all seemed well. However, two major events went against me: 1) the Botswana economy really slowed down and access to finance tightened, hence the housing market came to a grinding halt with values dropping by as much as 20% in some areas and 2) the development took a year and a half longer than expected to complete, as a number of people pulled out of the purchases and the developer's finances tightened.

Whilst I did not make a loss per se, it tied up my capital for a while and did not given me the gains I could have had in other investments.

It was not all doom and gloom despite the challenges faced, as buying this property was akin to getting a university degree in residential development. I learned a lot both from the pros and cons perspective and the lessons learnt will be a big asset in any future developments I get involved in.

5. OVERSTRETCHING YOUR FINANCES AND MORTGAGE PAYMENTS (POOR CASHFLOW MANAGEMENT)

Overstretching your finances and mortgage payments (whether for a buy-to-own or buy-to-let property) is a dangerous mistake and should be avoided. You must have heard the old cliché that '*cash is king*'. It really is. **In fact, cash is king, queen, prince charming and the whole kingdom.**

There are successful businesses that have gone under due to not managing their cash flow. According to preferredcfo.com, 82% of small business fail due to poor cash flow management. Also, according to simplybusiness.co.uk poor cash management is one of the top five reasons for business failure.

You could buy the perfect property with great potential for value growth but if you cannot meet the mortgage payments and other expenses, you may go into debt default and/or be forced the sell the property. Instead of making a profit, you may end up taking a big loss. It is better to buy a less expensive property that you can afford rather than overstretching and putting your financial health at risk.

6. OVERPAYING FOR PROPERTY

There is something known as the 'winners curse' and whilst the concept applies more in auctions, the same principle can be applicable in any purchase if you get emotional and overpay for something. According to Investopedia.com:

"The winner's curse is a tendency for the winning bid in an auction to exceed the intrinsic value of the item purchased. Because of incomplete information, emotions or any other number of factors regarding the item being auctioned, bidders can have a difficult time determining the item's intrinsic value."

As a property buyer, you should avoid emotion creeping in so that you can make a sensible and informed decision on the purchase. This applies whether you are buying the property for yourself or as an investment. The moment you let emotion come into the deal, you open the door to make poor financial decisions.

If you overpay for a property you will not only affect your cash flow, as you will have higher interest payments, but you will also reduce the returns on your property when you sell it (as you will have lower profit).

Overpayment is, in fact, very common in competitive property markets such as in Auckland and Sydney where it is difficult to get a foot in the door. According to domain.com.au; below are five key reasons why buyers tend to overpay for property:

a) Buying with your heart instead of your head (i.e. letting emotion come into play)
b) Making on-the-spot decisions without doing enough research on a property
c) Not seeking professional advise e.g. from lawyers, building inspectors, etc.
d) Buying into the hype of a property
e) Not sticking to plan at an auction and getting carried away

7. BUYING THE WRONG PROPERTY

When you purchase a property, there are various transaction costs involved. In countries that have stamp duty tax, the transaction costs can be as high as 10%. So if you purchase the wrong property due to being in a rush or buying into the hype of the property, you end up with something that is not right for your current needs. This may, in turn, result in you incurring unnecessary transaction costs if you have to sell the property to buy the right one.

8. TRYING TO MANAGE PROPERTY YOURSELF IF YOU DO NOT HAVE THE RIGHT SKILLS AND EXPERIENCE

Managing a property requires knowledge and skills. As highlighted in Chapter 9, a property manager plays a critical role. If you do not have the necessary time to learn about managing your property, and then to actively manage the property, then it is best that you hire a good property manager; otherwise, although you may save come costs in the short run, you may actually end up losing money in the long run.

9. HIRING THE WRONG PROPERTY MANAGERS

As per my personal story in Chapter 9, hiring the wrong property manager can not only cause you major headaches but also result in you losing income and incurring more costs. So make sure you are comfortable with your property manager, and if they are not performing, change to a better one as soon as possible.

10. NOT MAINTAINING YOUR PROPERTY

If you do not adequately maintain your property, it could affect your rental returns as it may look run down and not attract a high enough rent. It could also result in much higher replacement costs if you do not proactively service things such as boilers and spouts.

11. OVER CAPITALISING YOUR PROPERTY

Adding value to your property in a sensible way is a great idea as it can increase your rental returns and increase the value of the asset. However, over capitalisation is not a good idea, as you may not get the returns for the investment and the money may be much better spent elsewhere. E.g. by spending $100,000 on improving your kitchen or adding a fourth bathroom may not necessarily increase the value of the house by this amount – so you should ask yourself if it is necessary and whether a smaller investment could give you a balanced outcome between improved living conditions and value increase.

12. NOT HAVING THE RIGHT INSURANCE FOR YOUR PROPERTY

If you do not appropriately insure your property, you could lose substantial money if any major issues arise. The key types of insurance to focus on are building insurance, contents insurance and rental protection insurance. So, seek professional advice and be confident that you are properly insured.

13. NOT DOING YOUR FINANCIAL RETURNS CORRECTLY OR ON TIME

It is critical that you have a clear view of your financial performance, not only to file your annual tax returns, but to also have a clear idea of how your asset(s) is/are performing. You could be liable for major penalties if you do not correctly file your tax returns. You could also end up in financial trouble if you do not have a clear view of the status of your cash flow and how your investment is performing.

14. NOT FIRMING UP COSTS EARLY IN A DEVELOPMENT CONTRACT

When you are building a new property or making major extensions, it is critical that you firm up the costs earlier rather than later. Developers or construction companies love to put a number of unknown costs under what they call 'Provisional Sums' or 'PC Sums' (e.g. for building foundations and drainage). In theory this is a sensible approach, given that the constructors do not have a clear idea about this without doing some upfront work, and so they estimate these and then adjust as necessary. It is far better to pay them upfront to do whatever research is required and then to have a fixed cost, else you could be in for some serious surprises.

When I undertook a new build in New Zealand, I was conscious of this and so I negotiated with the contractor to only pay them a fixed margin for the PC Sums so that they would not be incentivised to increase these in order to make more money. However, I still ended up with a cost overrun of over 10%. In hindsight, it would have been better to have paid them upfront to do whatever research they required so that I could have had a fully fixed cost contract.

15. NOT GETTING MULTIPLE QUOTES FOR MAJOR WORKS DEVELOPMENTS

Never be in such a hurry that you cannot get multiple quotes for a major piece of work, otherwise you will be at the mercy of the single company you go with. You will not have a clear idea of whether you've overpaid, and you will also have no leverage to negotiate at the outset.

Because I was not living in New Zealand when I undertook my first development, I was in a rush to find a developer and after talking to a few potential parties, I picked a reputable company as I wanted someone reliable, even if they were a bit more expensive. However, not only did the project overrun by almost a year, I also ended up incurring over 10% additional costs as noted earlier. In hindsight, there was no point of rushing and it would have been better to get at least 2-3 quotes. C'est la vie! We learn from our mistakes!

CHAPTER 14: MANAGING YOUR FINANCES AND FILING TAX RETURNS

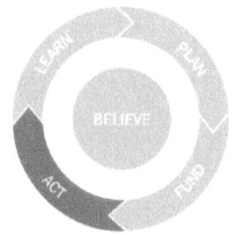

THE IMPORTANCE OF MANAGING YOUR FINANCES AND TAXES

It goes without saying that it is critical to have a clear view of your finances and to file your taxes correctly. Not tracking your financial position is like going on a journey but not knowing where you are or where you are going. It is fine if you are on holiday and have nothing better to do but in real life, with real business, it is not a good idea.

And filing your taxes correctly is not only good for your business but it keeps the lawman happy. Do not take shortcuts. Track your revenue, your expenses and keep your invoices. Also, unless you have lots of time to spare and have a lot of experience in filing your own taxes, get a good accountant to do your returns. If you think you will save money by not having a good accountant, then all I can tell you is to wake up — you will not save any money — at least not in the long run. Just like the way you get a capable plumber to do your plumbing at home and a good mechanic to fix your car (particularly in modern times where everything is electronic and not simple like it used to be!), use a good accountant to file your tax returns.

One of the best recommendations I ever read was to find a good accountant and a good lawyer. I have, therefore, always tried to follow this advice and it has not let me down.

THE IMPORTANCE OF MANAGING YOUR CASHFLOW

As highlighted in the 'Common Mistakes' section, managing your cash flow is critical. On paper you could be making money, but cash is what matters at the end of the day. So really watch your cash position and ensure that you have sufficient reserves to cover your mortgage, monthly expenses and have a buffer for any unforeseen issues, e.g. a hot water cylinder blowing in one of your properties.

KEEPING TRACK OF YOUR INCOME AND EXPENSES

If you have a good property manager, they will do a pretty good job of tracking both your income and expenses for you (i.e. the amounts that go through them).

Ask your property manager to give you an annual returns statement for each property and for the overall portfolio. Also ensure that they provide invoices for any expenses incurred.

The way I manage this is by having a folder for each financial year and I keep a copy of all invoices. For any expenses incurred via my property manager, I ask her to provide these for each financial year. I also have a spreadsheet that I use to track both my inflows and outflows and I use this as a basis for doing my annual tax returns. I also get summary statements for each property from my property manager.

FILING YOUR ANNUAL RETURNS

I find it a pain to file my annual tax returns, as I have to get all my paperwork in order and pass it on to my accountant. It then takes work to review everything and ensure that the accountant's numbers align with the numbers I have done at my end. BUT I know that I have no choice and this needs to be done, otherwise the tax man will not be happy.

Be sure to keep all paperwork relating to your financial returns for a minimum of seven years, or per government regulation in your country, as you could be audited at any time. The audit may require you to present documentation going as far back as regulation demands in your country.

SECTION D - OTHER IMPORTANT MATTERS

I am not a teacher, but an awakener.

-Robert Frost

CHAPTER 15: BELIEVING AND OTHER SPIRITUAL ASPECTS

BELIEVE THAT YOU CAN ACHIEVE YOUR DESIRES

I am a staunch believer of *believing*. If you do not believe that you can do something, then the likelihood of you actually making that thing happen is virtually zero. Let us think of a few examples here.

If you do not believe that you can run a marathon, will you run one? I doubt it. Firstly, you will not put in the hours of practice, secondly, even if you try to do so, there will be one stumbling block or another (e.g. injuries, bad weather, other excuses to not train enough, etc.).

If you do not believe that you can earn a salary of $200,000 then will you apply for jobs that pay that much? Will you ask for that level of salary at your current job? The answers to both these questions are "no". However, if you believe you are worth $200,000, then you will first seek the relevant qualifications and experience, you will strive for promotions and you will find the jobs that pay that kind of money and you will eventually go for them! It is not guaranteed that you will indeed get the exact target you have had in mind, but at least you will be far better off than someone who does not believe at all.

You must believe you can do something to make something happen. Believing is the first step in achieving anything. **Believing has the power to transform dreams to realities!**

AIM HIGH

A very good lesson I learnt from the book *The Magic of Thinking Big*, which I would strongly recommend that you read, was that it is not about the CONTENT but the CONTEXT.

I follow a simple philosophy: "Aim for the stars and at least you will reach the sky". If you aim low, then you will achieve low. If you aim high, then you stand a very good chance of reaching a very good level even if you do not reach exactly where you would have liked to.

If your objective is to achieve a low-level managerial role and to live in an average 3-bed home in an average suburb, then it is likely that this is what you will achieve. You will have a small "wish bucket" and you will have filled it. On the other hand, someone with a very *large* "wish bucket", who aims very high, might have the objective to become the CEO of a company or to own their own successful business, to own a luxury villa in a very expense suburb and to have many other investment properties. Even if this person only achieves half of his or her objectives, they will be far better off than the person who aims low.

The point of the above example is that you should position yourself for roles and investments that pay well so that your effort is worth it. Now if you are thinking that you do not have the qualifications or skills to be a CEO or an entrepreneur, then I would refer you to the 'Believe' section of this chapter. Believe you can achieve what you want to achieve, set goals and then break them down to achieve them!

SURROUND YOURSELF WITH POSITIVE, LIKE-MINDED PEOPLE

You should try to associate yourself and spend time with like-minded people who are positive and who believe that they can make things happen. If you surround yourself with pessimistic people who are always thinking of the negative, then you will surround yourself with doubt and negativity and severely reduce your chances of succeeding. If your friends and close associates are either already successful or who want to be successful, then you have a much higher chance to be successful yourself.

Additionally, if you want to make money from property, then liaise and network with people who share that interest. In the book *Think and Grow Rich*, the author describes that success is often achieved when like-minded people discuss a problem and find solutions together. By spending time with people who are interested in property investing, you are going to be in a much better position to learn new things, come across opportunities, share challenges and discuss potential solutions, co-invest, et cetera.

AFFIRMATIONS

According to www.dictionary.com an affirmation is *"a statement or proposition that is declared to be true."*

I am not going to pretend to possess any expertise in this area but one thing that has always worked for me when I have applied it correctly is affirmations. I was initially very sceptical about these but trust me, they somehow work. It is like what a chiropractor recently told me about acupuncture — the science world does not fully understand how it works but it just does. So do it!

You will see that I have recommended Joe Vitale's *Law of Attraction* in the readings section. This book highlights five key steps to attract anything in life but the book is focused on attracting wealth. You will find a lot more information on affirmations and what he calls 'Nevillising' in his book.

MEDITATION & BEING IN THE NOW

Our lives today are very hectic, and we deal with a lot of stress on a daily basis. We look after our interests, our hobbies, and even our bodies but often, we forget to look after our minds.

If we make an effort to better look after our minds, we can have better clarity around our objectives and how to achieve them. We often waste time ruminating on the past and / or planning for the future instead of being in the moment and living in the now. We also create beliefs that we can't do this or that simply because we've failed at it in the past or because something in our childhood put that belief in our mind (e.g. our parents' beliefs).

I started actively meditating about one year ago and it has changed my life and the way I look at everything. The reason I started meditating and reading books associated with this is because I was stressed and sometimes in an anxious state. I have always been a deep thinker, with a very analytical mind (which certainly has many benefits); however, the downside is that one can overthink and over analyse and either live in the past or spend a lot of time planning for the future. The end result of this is that we forget the 'Now' and forget to enjoy the current moment and let life pass us by. Meditation has really helped me to focus on the now and to appreciate what I have now rather than merely chasing the next dream. This does not mean that one should not think about the past as a learning tool or plan for

the future (which this book talks a lot about), but there are times
for this and it should be done in a manageable way.

Below are some Smart Phone applications and books I would strongly recommend to anyone who wants to appreciate the 'now' and reduce stress and anxiety.

SMART PHONE APPLICATIONS

1. CALM
2. HEADSPACE
3. SATVA

BOOKS

1. *The Power of Now* by Eckhart Tolle
2. *Breathing – The Master Key to Self-Healing* by Andrew Weil. M.D.
3. *The Art Of Breathing* – By Dr Danny Penman
4. *A Life Worth Breathing*: *A Yoga Master's Handbook of Strength, Grace and Healing* by Max Strom
5. *The Worry-Free Mind* by Carol Kershaw and Bill Wade

THE BENEFITS OF READING AND EXAMPLES OF SOME GREAT READINGS

I am an avid reader and I cannot even begin to describe what I have learned from my readings and the achievements that I have had as a result. What I learnt at school and university is probably less than a quarter of what I know. The rest has come through learning from others, through real life experiences and through many self-help books.

When people say that they do not have time for reading, it truly amazes me. Reading opens so many new doors and saying that you do not have time for reading is like a child saying that they do not have time to go to school. If you read, learn and grow, you will literally create more time for yourself and you will learn to do more in a shorter time by acquiring more knowledge.

Below is a short list of more amazing books that I have read, and these have helped me tremendously. These days I tend to listen to audio books rather than read in written format, as it allows me to read a lot more than I previously could, e.g. while driving or being on the tube.

1. *Think and Grow Rich* by Napoleon Hill - This book is a *must read* for anyone wanting to become wealthy. It is an old book but has great ideas that are still very much applicable today and I, in fact, found that a lot of other self-help books are based on key concepts from it.

2. *You Are a Bad Ass* by Jen Sincero - This is one of my favourite books and Jen has an incredible style. She talks about how you can achieve your goals and realise your potential in a very holistic way. Honestly, just buy this book read it — it is a no brainer.

3. *The Ultimate Law of Attraction* by Joe Vitale - Joe is an incredible personality and an inspiration. This book combines different talks focused on attracting wealth in your life. The main theme of this book is based on five key steps that help you attract anything you want in life.

4. *The Secret of Attracting Money* by Joe Vitale - This book is similar to the one above with complete focus on attracting money in your life.

5. *The Secret* by Rhonda Byrne & *The Power* by Rhonda Byrne - These books make you realise that there are deeper ways in which you can influence your life beyond what you can control with your conscious mind. Read these!

6. *The Magic of Thinking Big* by David Schwartz - This book is a game changer as it questions what goals you set and

makes you focus on setting big goals and achieving big. This book truly is a must-read.

7. *The Chimp Paradox* by Prof Steve Peters - This book totally blew me away and for the first time I realised how my mind actually works. It splits your brain into three parts: The human brain, the chimp brain and the computer. Seriously, just buy this book now, as it will make you appreciate and understand your brain, which ultimately drives your whole life and your relationships.

8. *Rich Dad Poor Dad* by Robert Kiyosaki - This was the first book I ever read on getting wealthy and it made me realise that books can actually change the way you think. Before this book, I only read novels and biographies!

9. *Black Box Thinking* by Matthew Syed - This book is focused on explaining why failure is important in helping achieve ultimate success. It uses the example of the airline industry, where there is a huge focus on being transparent with mistakes and using these to make it a better and safer industry.

10. *The 5 Second Rule* by Mel Robbins - This book describes a simple five-second rule that can help you change your default reactions, e.g. if you struggle to get out of bed in the morning when the alarm rings, count down from five to one and then just get up before your mind has the time to think of anything else! This idea has genuinely started helping me in a number of areas where I sometimes procrastinate.

So, if we link the learnings from the above books to property investing, the point is to believe and take action without the fear of making mistakes. It is better to do and fail rather than sit back and watch life pass you by! Even if you do fail, you will have learned something important which you can then apply to your next investment!

CHAPTER 16: BASIC PRINCIPLES OF NEGOTIATION

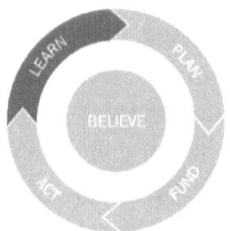

Many of you may think that you are not great negotiators and that it takes someone with natural skills to be good at negotiating. Well, natural skills can help, but negotiation is a skill like any other and it can definitely be learnt.

According to Harvard's Program on Negotiation:

"Negotiation is a deliberative process between two or more actors that seek a solution to a common issue or who are bartering over an item of value. Negotiation skills include the range of negotiation techniques negotiators employ to create value and claim value in their deal-making business negotiations and beyond. Negotiation skills can help you make deals, solve problems, manage conflicts, and build relationships as well as preserve relationships. Negotiation skills can be learned with conscious effort and should be practiced once learned."

Key principles to apply when undertaking any negotiation are listed below. These principles can also apply during a salary negotiation.

PREPARE

Before you enter any negotiation, you must prepare, prepare and prepare. You need to know what you want to achieve and what the other party may want to achieve. You need to know how you will go about the negotiation process in terms of strategy and where you will stop.

KNOW YOUR IDEAL OUTCOME AND THE WORST OUTCOME YOU ARE WILLING TO ACCEPT

You must know what your ideal, and what the worst possible outcome you are willing to accept is, so that you can have a sensible negotiation. If you achieve the ideal outcome, then great; however, if the negotiation gets tough and the other party is not moving, you need to know the worst outcome that you are willing to accept before walking away from the deal. A very important thing that I learnt is that there is no deal in this world that is too good to walk away from. If you bear that in mind, then it will help keep emotion out of the negotiation.

KNOW WHAT THE OTHER PARTY'S DESIRED OUTCOME IS

Ideally, it can also be very advantageous if you know what the other party's desired outcome is. This can be very difficult to know in many negotiations but as you negotiate you start to get a feel for what the other party's expectations are.

DETERMINE IF THERE IS A ZONE OF POTENTIAL OVERLAP (ZOPA)

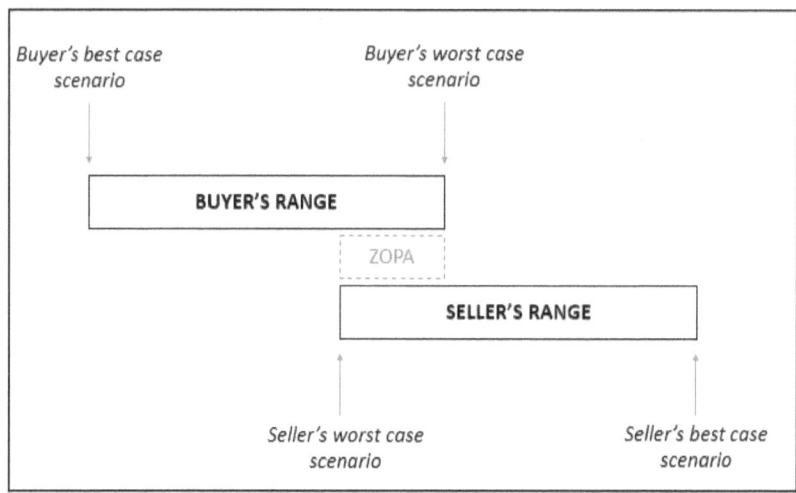

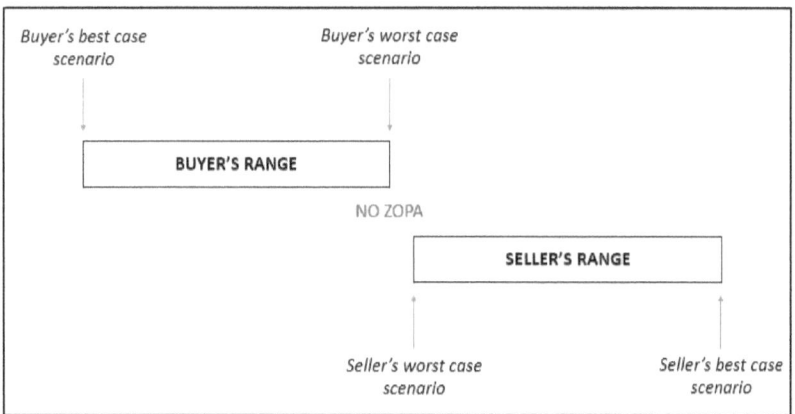

Let us take a situation where you see a house advertised at $1,000,000. Let us assume that it is a private deal and is not an auction. You want to make an offer. You know that the ideal purchase price would be $950,000 but you would be willing to pay up to $980,000. In essence, there is a $30,000 bargaining range.

From the seller's perspective, they may be willing to accept a price as low as $960,000 but their ideal outcome may be $990,000.

For someone willing to offer only as high as $950,000 there would be no deal as there is no common ZOPA. However, in your case there is an overlap between that highest price you are willing to offer and the seller's lowest acceptable price. If you agree on a deal of $960,000, you would be $20,000 better off compared to your worst-case outcome and the buyer would have still achieved their minimum asking price.

SET AN ANCHOR

Anchoring is a way for you to give a perception of your ZOPA to the other party. Some people can be very aggressive with their anchor (e.g. asking for a very high discount, say 40%), but this can cause the other party to question your credibility and your seriousness about the transaction. On the other hand, if this is done in a smart way, it can achieve very powerful results. Harvard's Program on Negotiation gives very good examples on this as below:

"A job applicant may state his belief that people with his qualifications tend to be paid between $85,000 and $95,000 annually, or he might mention that a former colleague just received an offer of $92,000. This assertion is not an offer; it's an anchor that affects the other side's perceptions of the ZOPA."

"A prospective customer might tell a salesperson that, while he loves the product, his purchasing department is undoubtedly going to demand price cuts of 15% or more."

HAVE A BEST ALTERNATIVE TO NEGOTIATED AGREEMENT (BATNA)

A BATNA is very important. This is because it gives you more power in a negotiation, as you can walk away from the negotiation. Having a BATNA keeps emotion away and enables you to achieve the best possible deal.

Let us take an example of a property purchase. You come across a property you like and manage to agree a purchase price of $900,000 but you include some conditions that can enable you to walk away from the deal. You then come across a second, very good property priced at $920,000, and you decide to put an offer for it. You can put a more aggressive offer, say of $880,000, given that you can use the other deal to leverage your position. If it is a buyers' market and the seller realises that you have a strong BATNA and can walk away from the deal, he/she may be more willing to concede.

If you do not have a BATNA, then you have less leverage and if you really want the deal you may be forced to accept a deal that is more towards your worst-case outcome, or even worse, if you've become emotional about the purchase or sale.

In general, you should always be willing to walk away from a deal. This ensures that you do not get emotionally involved and get a bad outcome.

NEGOTIATE ON MULTIPLE ITEMS RATHER THAN ON ONE THING AT A TIME

Another critical negotiation technique is to negotiate on multiple items. When you are buying a property, you may think that the only item to negotiate on with the seller is the price (or vice versa if you are the seller). That is not quite right.

For example, a seller of a property may have special needs around the timing of the property, say if their family is moving overseas and they still need the house for another three months so that the family is not inconvenienced by moving to another temporary property. As the buyer, you could be willing to agree to this requirement provided that the seller agrees a certain price. There could also be other items as part of the negotiation — such as repairs. If you bundle these items together and negotiate simultaneously on them, it makes the negotiation richer and allows for more avenues for a mutual agreement to be reached.

This technique can be very powerful as you could include certain non-essential requirements as a very strong preference, but later concede on these, e.g. the timing of the property exchange, and then make the other party feel that they have won in some areas. In the above example of the buyer's need to keep the house for three months, you could imply that this is very hard for you due to certain needs at your end, e.g. you child's schooling, but later be willing to concede on this provided that the buyer drops the price.

KNOW WHEN TO QUIT

It is important to keep an objective view of the situation and to judge when you need to accept the deal rather than to keep pushing, E.g. if the vendor has proposed a figure that is within your range of an acceptable deal, then certainly try to push for more if you think it is appropriate; however, know when to quit pushing so that you do not upset the other party and totally lose out on a potentially good deal.

NEGOTIATE IN A PROFESSIONAL AND POLITE MANNER

Keep a good relationship with the other party and negotiate in a professional and polite manner. Do not turn it into a situation where the other party walks away from the deal because they get emotional and upset with you. Also, you will find it easier to achieve your desired outcome if you find a way for the other party to also feel that they somehow won on some front (e.g. timing of payment rather than the amount). Also, avoid lying when you negotiate; otherwise you may be caught and again lose out on the deal and end up with a broken relation and a potentially damaged reputation.

If you are in a one-off negotiation with a party, then you can be more aggressive with your demands and less focused on maintaining a relationship (e.g. when purchasing a house from a stranger). You might even get away by exaggerating your BATNA; however, where you have an on-going relationship (e.g. with a tradesman who does maintenance work for you) you need to ensure that you do not offend the other party and destroy the relationship you have and/or negatively impact future deals.

USE HELP

Using help during a negotiation can be very fruitful, e.g. in getting a better feel for the other party's ZOPA, or to act as the go between. In the case of a property transaction, the real estate agent can play a critical role. When you give your offer (including any bundled items) the agent presents this to the seller on your behalf. This avoids conflict and any emotion creeping into the negotiation as the agent is a neutral party and a mere messenger.

CHAPTER 17: ALTERNATIVE WAYS TO GET EXPOSURE TO THE REAL ESTATE MARKET

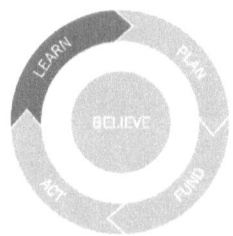

If you find that, despite testing every avenue to fund your property venture, you have fallen short of your goal, but you still want exposure to the property market, there are other options available. Some of these options are as follows:

1. INVEST IN A REAL ESTATE FUND

These are known as Real Estate Investment Trusts (or REITS). According to www.REIT.com

"A REIT, or Real Estate Investment Trust, is a company that owns or finances income-producing real estate. Modelled after mutual funds, REITs provide investors of all types regular income streams, diversification and long-term capital appreciation. REITs typically pay out all of their taxable income as dividends to shareholders. In turn, shareholders pay the income taxes on those dividends."

REITs tend to be run by large, established institutions and they are generally targeted at commercial property but there are a few REITs that also invest in residential property (e.g. American Housing Income Trust, Inc. (NASDAQ: AHIT)). Different REITs tend to specialise in specific sectors (e.g. Office blocks, Retail, Residential, etc.).

Most REITS are listed companies on major stock exchanges but there are other forms of REITS such as Private REITS.

The 2 types of REITS are:

a. Equity REITs — equity investments in properties and get returns to rents and property sales. Investing in Equity REITs is like investing in the shares of a publicly listed company — the only difference is that an Equity REIT is targeted at investing in real estate and has special rules to follow.

b. Mortgage REITs — debt investments in properties and get returns through interest on property debt. Investing in a Mortgage REIT is similar to investing in government bonds, except a Mortgage REIT is specifically set up to fund real estate investments.

When you invest in a REIT you invest in the overall company rather than in a specific project as in the case of a Crowd Funding Platform described below.

Advantages:

- Diversified risk: You are not reliant on the growth of just one — or a handful of — properties, but rather on a broad and diverse portfolio.
- Professional management: The properties are managed by experts who are highly skilled and experienced in property investments.

- Liquid investment: You can sell your shares whenever you want.
- High dividends: As it is a key criterion for REITs to give back 90% of returns as dividends.
- Secure income: As income is obtained through long-term commercial leases.

Disadvantages:

- Lack of direct control, i.e. you have no control over the investments.
- Slow growth of fund value, as only 10% of returns are invested back (the rest of the returns are returned to investors as dividends).
- Tax implications (see http://marketrealist.com/2015/08/advantages-disadvantages-investing-reits/ for details on this)

Examples of REITs are as below:

- United States:
    - American Housing Income Trust, Inc. (NASDAQ: AHIT)
    - Boston Properties, Inc. (NYSE: BXP)
    - Brandywine Realty Trust (NYSE: BDN)
- UK
    - British Land Company (BLND)
    - Land Securities (LAND)
    - Secure Income REIT (SIR)
    - Supermarket Income REIT (SUPR)
- Australia
    - Goodman Group (ASX: GMG)
    - Westfield Corp Ltd (ASX: WFD)

- Scentre Group (ASX: SCG)
- New Zealand:
  - AMP Property Trusts - (NZ)
  - Argosy Property Trust - (ARG)
  - Tower Mortgage Plus Fund - (NZ)

2. INVEST WITH A REAL ESTATE CROWD FUNDING PLATFORM

Real estate crowd funding has revolutionised the industry both for investors and borrowers. It enables projects to flourish in situations where they would have conventionally not been able to take off due to funding constraints.

According to www.finder.com.au, real estate crowdfunding allows a large group of investors to pool their funds in order to back a project, in this case a development or investment property.

Real estate crowd funds benefit investors to invest in the real estate market and they benefit borrowers by allowing them to get peer-to-peer lending (i.e. an alternative to the traditional way of borrowing from banks).

The objective of real estate crowd funds is to:

- Enable investors who do not have sufficient funds to buy their own property (first or otherwise) to get exposure to the real estate market.
- Enable investors who do not want to actively find and manage property investments to invest in real estate,

There are many benefits for the investors:

- Access to the real estate market and types of projects that you would traditionally not be able to invest in — you can invest as little as a few hundred dollars in a given investment.

- Liquid investment compared to owning actual real estate, as you can trade your shares in the investment.

- You can choose the type of investment to get involved in and the level of risk versus return involved in that investment.

- Returns can be very attractive — much higher than cash deposits — and in some cases even higher than in the share market.

- Your credit history is not impacted if any investment goes pear shaped.

- It enables you to learn about real estate investments through hands-on experience in investing in projects of your choice.

CHAPTER 18: CASE STUDY — A DEEP DIVE INTO THE NEW ZELAND PROPERTY MARKET

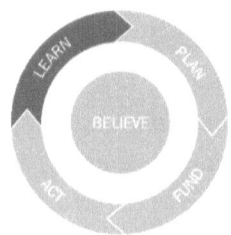

This section's objective is to serve as a case study with a deep dive into a specific real estate market.

Even if you are not a New Zealander you may find this section an interesting read and gain knowledge from it that could apply to your own situation. I would therefore highly encourage you to read it.

I have chosen New Zealand for the case study, as it has had some of the highest property price growths in the past few years and property in several cities now appears overpriced. Millennials and post millennials in New Zealand are amongst those who are most feeling the pinch in buying their first property. It serves as a good example for you to do a deeper study of the property market in your own country and/or city. Similar, broader principles will apply regardless of where you invest.

OVERVIEW

Let us start with some basic facts about New Zealand and why it is not only a great place to live but also a good place to invest in. Below are some key facts according to newzealandnow.govt.nz:

- It has a great lifestyle — there is a good sense of work and life balance, and the overall quality of life is very high. Auckland and Wellington are often listed amongst the top cities in the world in terms of quality of life by various lists, e.g. www.cntraveler.com lists Auckland in the top 10 places to live.
- It has a temperate climate and superb scenery.
- Overall cost of living is not atrocious — Auckland comes in at 98th and Wellington at 123rd most expensive cities to live in, according to Mercer's 2016 Cost of Living survey.
- In 2015, World Bank ranked New Zealand as the easiest place to start a business and the world's second easiest country in which to do business.
- The Heritage Foundation rated New Zealand the world's third freest economy in its 2015 Index of Economic Freedom, just behind Hong Kong and Singapore.
- New Zealand has a very export-driven, competitive economy with exports accounting for about 30% of GDP.
- Noting that New Zealand's economic growth has been faster than most other developed countries in recent years, the OECD commented in 2015 that: "inflation and inflation expectations are well anchored... Strong fiscal monetary policy frameworks and a healthy financial sector have yielded macroeconomic stability, underpinning growth. Employment is high, in large part thanks to flexible labour markets and ample immigration, business investment is robust, and households and firms are optimistic."

- The New Zealand Treasury forecast in May 2015 that New Zealand's economic growth would average 2.8% per year over the four years to 2019.

Its key cities are Auckland, Wellington and Christchurch. Other upcoming cities include Hamilton, Tauranga, Napier-Hastings, Dunedin and Palmerston North.

Auckland is by far the largest city and so it has the largest property market in New Zealand.

The value of residential dwellings (excluding chattels) is estimated at $1 trillion across New Zealand (RBNZ, 2017).

PRICE GROWTH IN THE PAST 25 YEARS

Based on Real Estate New Zealand data, the value of property for Auckland has multiplied by almost 7 times in the last 25 years and doubled in the last 5 years. Wellington and Christchurch property values have grown by 4 times in the past 25 years and by over 30% in the past 5 years.

The below chart (in Log scale*) shows property value growth compared to the Consumer Price Index; a measurement of inflation. We can see that property price growth has outpaced inflation. It has done so substantially in the recent years, hence the general fear in the market that there could be a bubble building up, particularly in Auckland.

*Note: A log scale shows how much a series has increased relative to its previous value, rather than its starting value. An increase of one index point represents a doubling in the index.

Figure 8: CONSUMER PRICE INDEX VS. NOMINAL HOUSE PRICES IN NEW ZEALAND - 1965 TO 2015 (Reserve Bank of New Zealand, Bulletin volume 79, 2016)

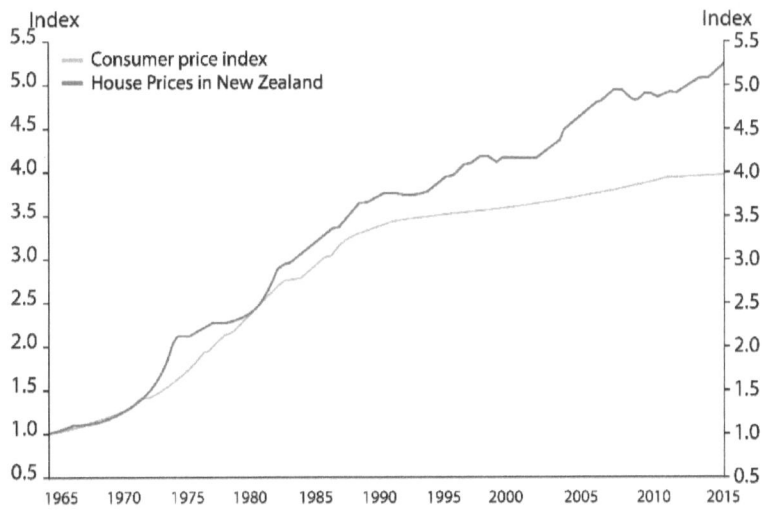

Despite fears of speculation being a key driver of the recent rapid property price growth in New Zealand, there are some solid underlying economic factors that have influenced the longer-term growth. These factors are as follows:

- Healthy GDP growth, which grew by an annual average of 2.6%
- Low interest rates
- High immigration

A DEEPER LOOK AT THE AUCKLAND PROPERTY MARKET AND GROWTH

The below chart shows the growth of Auckland property prices compared to the average New Zealand house price growth. The next chart shows the 10-year median house price trend in New Zealand compared to median income. From these charts we note that Auckland house prices have outpaced national house price growth and median wage growth.

Figure 9: AUCKLAND PRICE GROWTH COMPARED TO REST OF NEW ZEALAND - 2006 TO 2017 (QV, 2017)

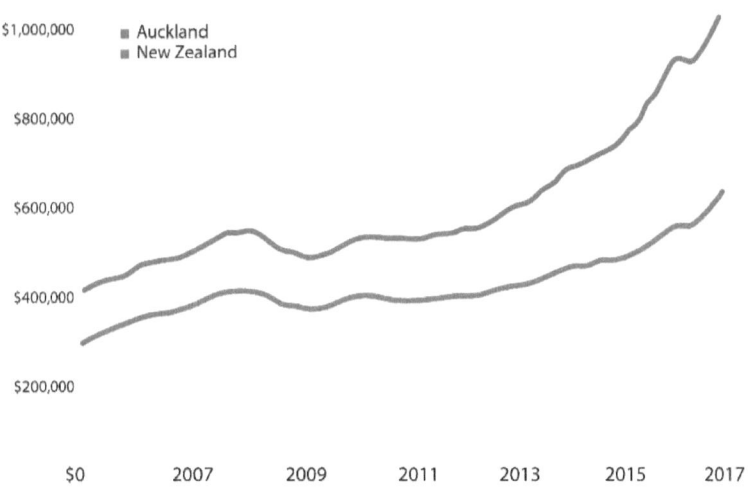

Figure 10: 10 YEAR TREND FOR AUCKLAND HOUSE PRICES VS MEDIAN INCOME - 2005 TO 2015 (NZ Hearald)

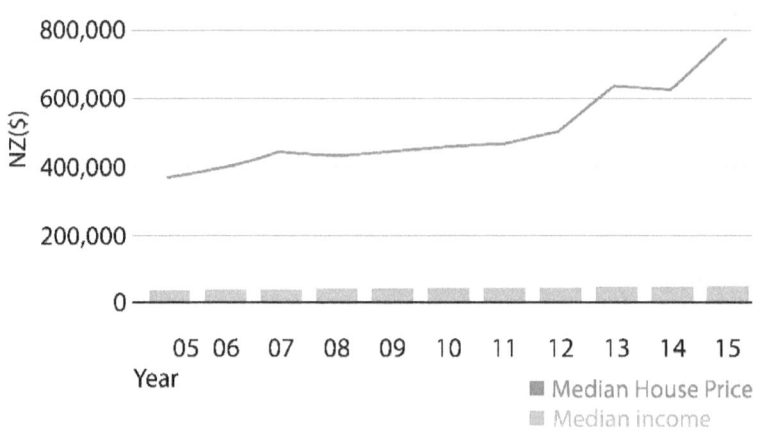

Some even went so far as to say that Auckland was the hottest property market in the world (when I started writing this book). However, as I am going through my first edit, prices have already softened due to the strict government regulation introduced to curb price growth. Some of the hot property markets as of early 2018 include Valencia, Spain and Montreal Canada according to Robb Report (http://robbreport.com).

The unique feature that have driven the growth of Auckland's property prices are as follows:

1. One third of New Zealand's population lives in Auckland. There are very few countries in the world where one third or more of the country's population lives in a single city.
2. It is a very popular city for New Zealanders due to its diversity, beauty and amenities and it has the most job opportunities.
3. It is often listed as one of the top-10 cities to live in the world due to its quality of life and other factors.
4. The growth of housing is not keeping up with the growth of the city's population; therefore, supply is outstripping demand and pushing up prices. The media and the government have blamed the council for having a long and restrictive consent process.
5. A large percentage of homes are reportedly owned by foreigners. Some estimate this number to be as high as 50%.
6. Property is seen as a key investment vehicle. Core Logic estimates that over a third of the buyers in 2012 were investors.

However, the main concern is that Auckland property prices are too high. According to some sources, Auckland has gone from the world's fifth least affordable city to fourth, now tailing only Hong Kong, Sydney and Vancouver as the least accessible housing market (NZ Herald, n.d.).

Whilst many reports seem to indicate the Auckland is now one of the most expensive cities in the world in terms of property, it depends on which sources and data you look at. E.g. according to globalpropertyguide.com, their research suggests that rental yields in New Zealand's prime cities are reassuringly high by international standards, and that, on this measure, New Zealand's high residential property prices are amply justified. Rents have been growing healthily and, in particular, very good yields can be achieved with apartments.

However, the fact does remain that Auckland property is expensive and there is a risk of a bubble. But if there is a property bubble in Auckland, then it is likely that there is a property bubble in many cities in the world, as residential property prices have skyrocketed in numerous major cities around the world and have showed no signs of coming down.

CURRENT PROPERTY VALUES

The August 2017 property median prices by regions were as below:

Figure 11: NEW ZEALAND MEDIAN HOUSE PRICES BY REGION - AUGUST 2017
(REINZ Residential Report, August 2017)

Northland	$428,000
Auckland	$840,000
Waikato	$480,000
Bay of Plenty	$538,000
Gisborne	$235,000
Hawke's Bay	$405,000
Manawatu/Wanganui	$285,000
Taranaki	$329,000
Wellington	$500,000
Nelson	$518,000
Marlborough	$420,000
Tasman	$496,000
West Coast	$185,000
Canterbury	$427,000
Otago	$380,000
Southland	$250,000
NZ excl. Auckland	**$428,000**
New Zealand	**$530,000**

The overall national average price had continued to climb in 2017 by 8.2%; however, Auckland had seen a drop of 1.2%

HOW DOES NEW ZEALAND COMPARE TO OTHER COUNTRIES IN THE WORLD?

PRICE GROWTH ANALYSIS

If we compare the property price growth of a few countries from 1980 to 2016, per the chart below, then New Zealand growth has clearly outpaced all other major countries.

Figure 12: HOUSE PRICE INDEX - SELECT COUNTRIES - 1980 TO 2016 (Global
House Prices - The Economist, 2017)

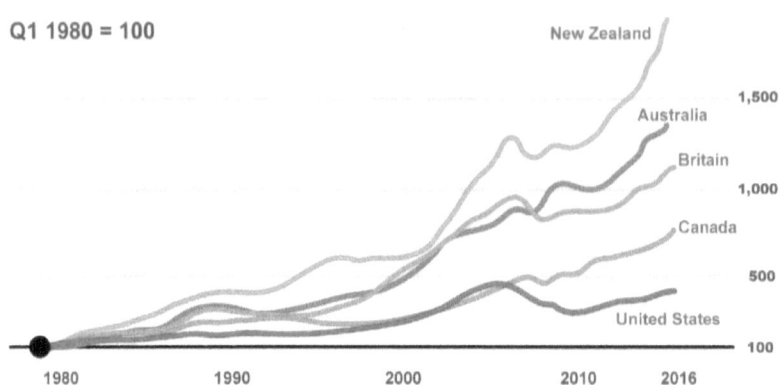

However, this picture can be misleading as New Zealand property
prices around the early 80s may have been undervalued. If we
look at a shorter time horizon of the past 16 years (i.e. since the
turn of the new millennium), then prices in many major countries
have more than doubled and the pace of growth has not been too
far from that of New Zealand. That said, New Zealand has still
had the highest growth of all, with values up by over three times.

Figure 13: HOUSE PRICE INDEX - SELECT COUNTRIES - 2000 TO 2016 (The Economist, 2017)

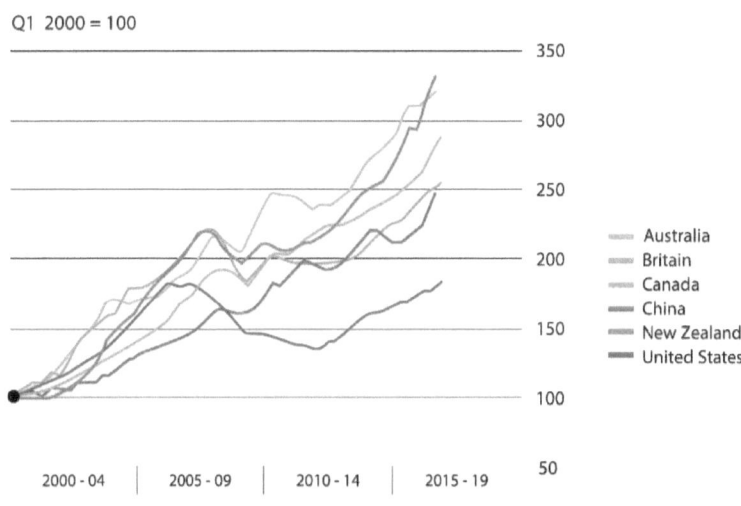

Sources: The Economist; OECD; ONS; Reserve Bank of New Zealand;
Standard s poor's; Teranet - National Bank; Thomson Reuters

PRICE-TO-INCOME RATIO ANALYSIS

We see a similar picture of growth when looking at price growth relative to income. The below chart shows house prices against average income, where 100 is the long-term average. House prices in Britain, Canada, Australia and New Zealand have outpaced income growth and New Zealand has had the largest relative growth.

Figure 14: PROPERTY PRICE RATIO RELATIVE TO INCOME IN SELECT COUNTRIES - 2000 TO 2016 (The Economist, 2017)

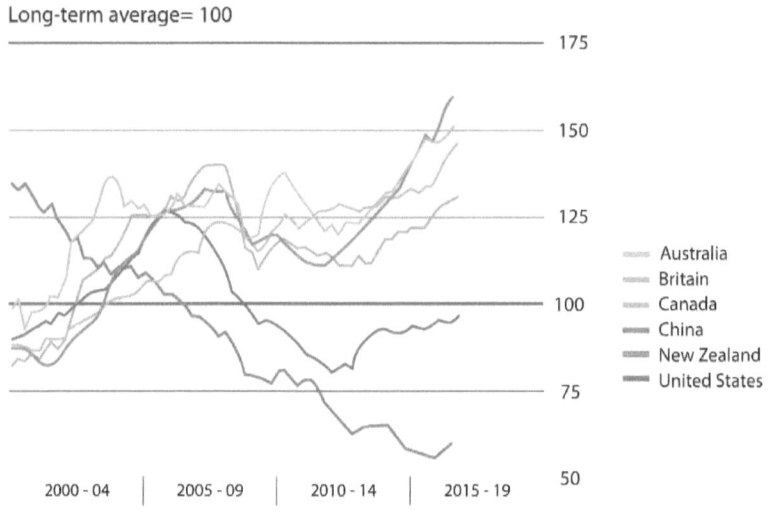

Sources: The Economist; OECD; ONS; Reserve Bank of New Zealand; Standard s poor's; Teranet - National Bank; Thomson Reuters

The below chart shows the property price-to-income index for a few more countries. Again, New Zealand leads the pack here in terms of property prices outpacing income growth.

Figure 15: HOUSE PRICE-TO-INCOME RATIO - 2010 TO 2016 (IMF, 2017)

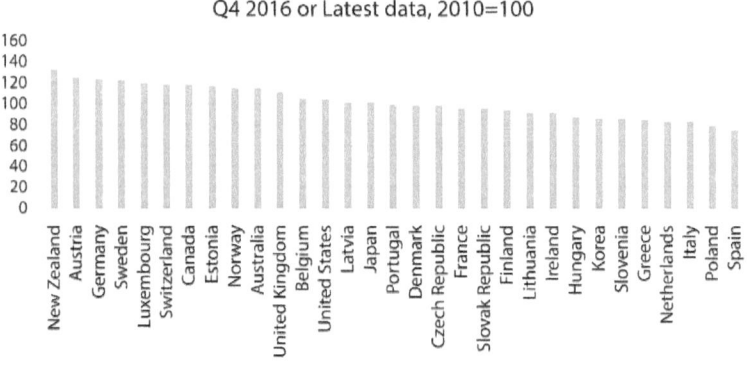

In terms of the overall ratio of property price-to-income ranking, rather than simply looking at recent growth, New Zealand comes in at 21 with a Property Price to Income Ratio of 8.14. In other words, the cost of the average property in New Zealand is 8.14 times the average household income. Hence New Zealand still appears to be an affordable country to purchase a home compared to many other countries in the world, if considered from an income perspective.

Figure 16: PROPERTY PRICE TO INCOME RATIO RANKING – 2017 (Numbeo, 2017)

Rank	Country	Price To Income Ratio	Gross Rental Yield City Centre	Gross Yield Outside Of centre	Price Rent Ratio City Centre	Price To Rent Ratio Outside Of City Centre	Mortgage As A Percentage Of Income	Affordability Index
1	Saudi Arabia	2.85	7.29	8.01	13.72	12.49	21.07	4.75
2	United States	3.26	11.23	12.24	8.90	8.17	23.53	4.25
3	South Africa	3.58	9.51	10.41	10.51	9.60	41.97	2.38
4	Libya	3.90	7.10	7.13	14.08	14.03	26.60	3.76
5	Puerto Rico	5.11	7.03	6.54	14.22	15.28	40.14	2.49
6	Cyprus	5.21	4.90	5.14	20.42	19.45	39.85	2.51
7	United Arab Emirates	5.60	9.70	10.65	10.30	9.39	42.07	2.38
8	Palestinian Territory	6.11	6.95	6.87	14.40	14.55	53.86	1.86
9	Iceland	6.15	8.07	8.37	12.39	11.95	57.70	1.73
10	Qatar	6.19	9.49	9.19	10.54	10.88	47.11	2.12
11	Canada	6.40	5.47	6.16	18.29	16.23	42.14	2.37
12	Mexico	6.94	6.85	6.31	14.60	15.85	86.58	1.16
13	Belgium	6.96	5.82	5.92	17.18	16.88	44.69	2.24
14	Ireland	7.02	6.02	6.91	16.61	14.48	50.79	1.97
15	Germany	7.46	3.75	4.09	26.62	24.47	45.91	2.18
16	Finland	7.60	3.74	4.60	26.72	21.76	44.51	2.25
17	Iraq	7.79	7.04	8.25	14.20	12.12	103.64	0.96
18	Norway	7.90	4.18	4.51	23.94	22.16	50.95	1.96
19	Jordan	7.96	6.48	7.23	15.43	13.84	76.63	1.30
20	Guatemala	8.05	7.25	8.56	13.80	11.68	94.38	1.06
21	New Zealand	8.14	4.99	5.92	20.04	16.90	63.92	1.56
22	Denmark	8.20	4.71	4.82	21.21	20.76	52.39	1.91
23	Namibia	8.20	10.09	9.24	9.91	10.83	100.90	0.99
24	Spain	8.26	4.38	5.23	22.81	19.13	52.02	1.92
25	Greece	8.33	4.14	4.20	24.15	23.80	62.48	1.60
26	Slovenia	8.34	4.20	4.21	23.82	23.77	60.26	1.66
27	Netherlands	8.52	5.38	5.95	18.68	16.86	56.24	1.78
28	Costa Rica	8.52	7.16	6.56	13.96	15.25	106.17	0.94
29	Malta	8.74	5.89	6.14	16.98	16.28	61.42	1.63
30	Portugal	8.85	5.95	6.08	16.81	16.46	60.87	1.64
31	Turkey	8.87	5.43	6.28	18.41	15.92	121.45	0.82
32	Bulgaria	9.07	5.36	5.68	18.65	17.59	77.24	1.29
33	Australia	9.24	4.90	5.05	20.41	19.82	70.87	1.41
34	Malaysia	9.53	4.07	4.05	24.60	24.66	72.87	1.37
35	Bolivia	9.65	6.03	6.76	16.58	14.79	89.13	1.12
36	Austria	9.66	3.63	3.78	27.55	26.46	59.08	1.69
37	Slovakia	9.85	5.62	5.57	17.78	17.94	61.59	1.62
38	United kingdom	10.00	4.16	4.40	24.02	22.75	69.10	1.45
39	Poland	10.12	4.66	5.25	21.44	19.04	73.08	1.37
40	India	10.28	3.08	3.81	32.44	26.24	123.44	0.81
41	Lativa	10.39	4.77	5.05	20.96	19.80	68.49	1.46
42	Estonia	10.54	4.11	3.95	24.33	25.30	68.75	1.45
43	Egypt	10.66	7.18	7.74	13.93	12.93	138.09	0.72
44	Chile	10.67	4.42	5.06	22.64	19.77	83.59	1.20
45	Czech Republic	10.70	4.17	4.61	24.01	21.71	65.37	1.53
46	Romania	10.79	4.89	4.76	20.43	20.99	83.30	1.20
47	Israel	10.87	3.45	3.54	28.98	28.27	71.94	1.39
48	Croatia	10.91	3.31	3.69	30.24	27.07	89.21	1.12
49	Hungary	11.20	5.43	5.57	18.43	16.76	97.32	1.03
50	Bosnia And Herzegovina	11.35	3.41	3.31	29.36	30.18	104.89	0.95

Additionally, as you can see from the chart below, it is Auckland's prices that skew the overall average values of New Zealand. Outside of Auckland, the price-to-income ratio is only 5.66, hence making other New Zealand cities far more affordable relative to incomes.

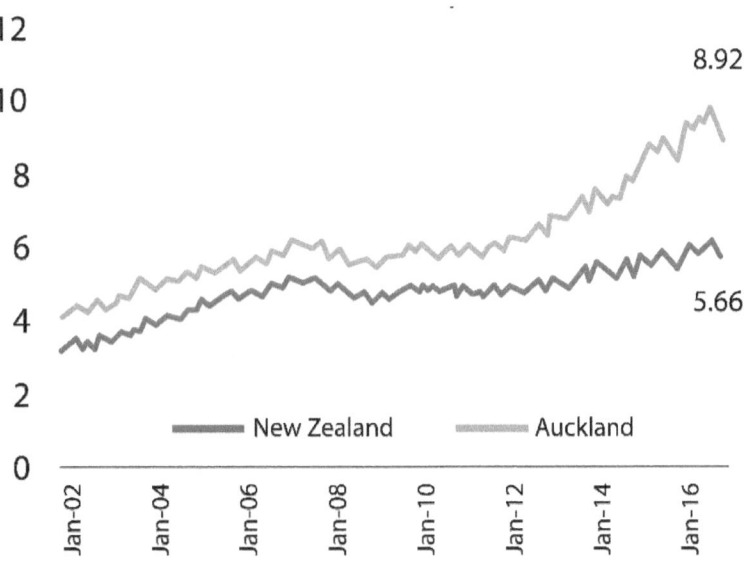

Figure 17: HOUSE PRICE TO INCOME RATIO FOR AUCKLAND AND NEW ZEALAND - 2002 TO 2016 (interest.co.nz, 2017)

The below table shows the median multiples by different cities. It gives you a very good idea of the affordability of buying a house in the different cities of New Zealand.

(interest.co.nz, 2017)

Dated 18 Apr 17	Population	Median House price	Median Household Income		
		Mar-17		Mar-17	Mar 16
NZ total	4,765,000	$546,000	$87,101	6.27	5.86
Whangarei	80,500	$362,500	$83,963	4.32	4.21
Auckland metro	1,486,000	$890,000	$90,766	9.81	9.32
- North Shore	225,800	$1,022,422	$96,219	10.63	10.08
- West	204,500	$786,558	$89,106	8.83	8.50

- Auckland Central	444,100	$1,082,974	$93,848	11.54	10.94
- South	368,500	$871,144	$84,602	10.30	8.78
Hamilton	145,600	$540,750	$83,367	6.49	5.84
Tauranga	115,700	$589,650	$81,425	7.24	6.48
Rotorua	68,900	$353,000	$83,125	4.25	3.35
Gisborne	46,600	$280,000	$75,111	3.73	3.19
Hastings	75,500	$420,000	$77,514	5.42	4.48
Napier	57,600	$395,375	$77,275	5.12	4.30
New Plymouth	73,800	$430,000	$80,645	5.33	4.57
Wanganui	43,500	$194,750	$76,868	2.53	2.31
Palmerston North	82,100	$320,000	$85,598	3.74	3.43
Wellington metro	487,700	$525,000	$94,426	5.56	5.01
- Kapiti Coast Dist.	48,900	$492,000	$82,622	5.95	4.90
- Porirua City	52,700	$560,000	$90,413	6.19	5.36
- Upper Hutt City	41,500	$436,250	$91,829	4.75	4.21
- Lower Hutt City	103,000	$460,000	$92,773	4.96	4.86
- Wairarapa	40,800	$322,500	$67,299	4.79	4.29
- Wellington City	200,100	$651,796	$105,049	6.20	5.54
Nelson	46,200	$483,250	$79,292	6.09	5.27
Christchurch	367,700	$486,320	$87,262	5.57	5.53
Timaru	44,700	$349,000	$81,526	4.28	3.95
Dunedin	126,000	$342,850	$73,932	4.64	4.25
Queenstown-Lakes	28,700	$897,500	$79,608	11.27	10.56
Invercargill	53,000	$230,000	$78,004	2.95	2.80

ANOTHER WAY OF LOOKING AT AFFORDABILITY OF BUYING PROPERTY IN NEW ZEALAND

The below diagrams show the affordability for an average first home buyer (aged 25–29) and young family buyers (aged 30-34) respectively, to buy a property in New Zealand and pay for the mortgage. The percentage figures indicated are the portion of the net income that the family would pay towards the mortgage.

The affordability is very reasonable compared to global standards, if you look outside of the Auckland region and Queenstown.

Mortgage payments are considered affordable when they take up no more than 40% of take home pay (www.interest.co.nz, 2017).

Refer to the website http://www.interest.co.nz/property/home-loan-affordability for notes and disclaimers in relation to these diagrams. You can also find the latest affordability data by region on this website.

Figure 18: FIRST HOME BUYER AFFORDABILITY INDEX FOR M AJOR NZ CITIES
(www.interest.co.nz, 2017)

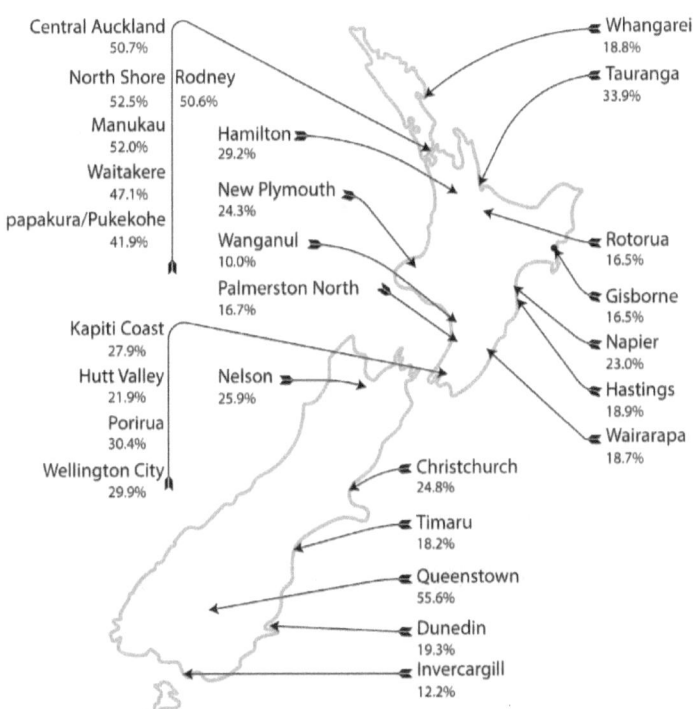

Figure 19: YOUNG FAMILY BUYER AFFORDABILITY INDEX FOR M AJOR NZ CITIES (www.interest.co.nz, 2017)

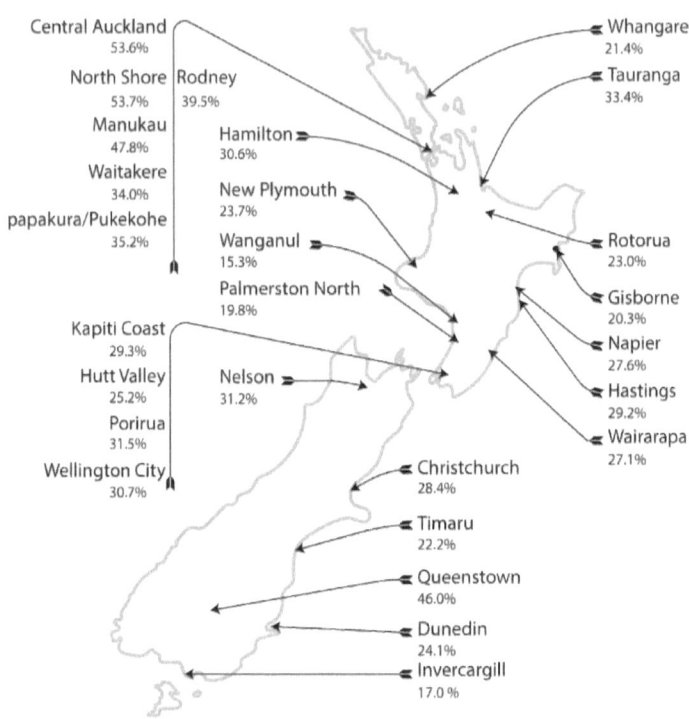

BENEFITS OF BUYING PROPERTY IN NEW ZEALAND

1. PROTECTION OF PROPERTY RIGHTS

According to www.heritage.org "The property rights component is an assessment of the ability of individuals to accumulate private property, secured by clear laws that are fully enforced by the state. It measures the degree to which a country's laws protect private property rights and the degree to which its government enforces those laws. It also assesses the likelihood that private property will be expropriated and analyses the independence of the judiciary, the existence of corruption within the judiciary, and the ability of individuals and businesses to enforce contracts.

"The more certain the legal protection of property, the higher a country's score; similarly, the greater the chances of government expropriation of property, the lower a country's score. Countries that fall between two categories may receive an intermediate score."

New Zealand's global ranking is third in the world. You can, therefore, have a very high level of confidence that your ownership rights are protected when you buy a property in New Zealand.

2. **EASE OF SETTING UP A BUSINESS AND RUNNING IT (IF YOU ARE AN INVESTOR).**

A key metric of economic success for a country is how easy is it to set up and run a business. According to Wikipedia: "The ease of doing business index is an index created by the World Bank Group. Higher rankings (a low numerical value) indicate better, usually simpler, regulations for businesses and stronger protections of property rights. Empirical research funded by the World Bank to justify their work show that the economic growth impact of improving these regulations is strong."

New Zealand was ranked number one in 2017. As an investor, it therefore a very attractive location in which to do business.

3. CAPITAL GAINS TAX APPLIES IN LIMITED SITUATIONS

Capital gains tax is the tax you pay on gains made on the value of the property at the time of selling it.

E.g. take the scenario where capital gains tax in a given country is 20% and you bought a house at $300,000 and sold it at $600,000

- Your capital gains are $600,000 - $300,000 = $300,000
- The tax you would therefore pay is 20% of $300,000 = $60,000

The above is a very simplistic scenario to convey the impact of capital gains tax. In reality, the calculation is more complex and there are situations where you may be exempt from it (e.g. in the UK and Australia, you do not pay capital gains tax on the sale of your primary home if certain conditions are met).

According to Deloitte, New Zealand does not have a general Capital Gains Tax. Such a tax only applies where the person or entity's primary purpose in acquiring property is for resale. New Zealand is one of the few developed countries where these favourable conditions apply. In most countries, only your primary home is exempt from this tax.

The IRD website states that:

"The tax you pay depends on four things

1. Your intent when you purchased.
2. Your history of buying and selling.
3. Whether you are in or associated with the property industry.
4. Whether you buy and sell a property within two years."

The IRD website provides further details around the situations where you may be liable for this tax. Follow this link for further details: http://www.ird.govt.nz/property/property-selling/selling-property.html

4. ABILITY TO OFFSET YOUR TAX AGAINST INTEREST PAID ON MORTGAGE

In New Zealand you can benefit from fully offsetting your tax at your marginal tax rate.

On the other hand, the UK recently changed its laws so that you cannot offset tax at your marginal tax rate against interest paid on mortgages. The lowest tax rate applies instead.

NZ Example: If your marginal tax rate is 40% and your interest payments per year are $10,000, then your tax savings will be 40% x $10,000 = $4,000 (as you would be able to deduct the $10,000 expense from your rental income before the calculation of tax). This assumes that your property makes over $10,000 net rental income after deducting other expenses.

UK Example: If your marginal tax rate is 40% and your interest payments per year are £10,000, then in the past your tax savings would have been 40% x £10,000 = £4,000 (as you would have been able to deduct the £10,000 expense from your rental income before the calculation of tax). This assumes that your property makes over £10,000 net rental income after deducting other expenses.

However, now the saving is based on the lowest tax rate, which is 20% x £10,000 = £2,000. There will, however, be a 3-year phased transition to this. (www.gov.uk, 2017).

5. NO STAMP DUTY TAX

So far, New Zealand does not require property buyers to pay a stamp duty. This is a very big benefit as stamp duty can add substantial upfront costs when you purchase property.

In the UK, for example, Stamp Duty Land Tax applies as below (www.gov.uk, 2017):

PROPERTY PURCHASE PRICE	SDLT RATE
Up to £125,000	Zero
The next £125,000 (the portion from £125,000 to £250,000)	2%
The next £675,000 (the portion from £250,000 to £925,000)	5%
The next £575,000 (the portion from £925,000 to £1.5 million)	10%
The remaining amount (the portion above £1.5 million)	12%

If you already own one or more properties, then you pay an additional 3% on top of the normal SDLT rates.

In Australia, stamp duty applies (apart from concessions to first time buyers in specific situations) and varies by state. For example, in New South Wales, a property purchase of $1,000,000 for a first-time buyer will incur a Stamp Duty Tax of AU$40,490 (www.yourmortgage.com, 2017).

6. SIMPLIFIED PURCHASE PROCESS WITH NO 'GAZUMPING'

New Zealand has a very simplified property purchase process. You make an offer to the buyer by completing a standard Property Sale and Purchase Agreement. You can indicate whether the agreement is conditional or non-conditional and the date at which the agreement becomes unconditional. Once the vendor signs this agreement, he/she cannot override your agreement unless you, as the buyer, decide to back off due to one of the conditions in the contract not being fulfilled. You can download the Sales and Purchase Agreement guide on the Real Estate Agents Authority website (http://www.reaa.govt.nz).

If you do specify conditions such as finance and due diligence, you can legitimately back off the transaction, e.g. if you find that the property has a very high risk of flooding as part of due diligence. If all conditions are satisfied and you get your finance in place, it is a fairly smooth process to execute the agreement and transfer the property.

On the other hand, in the UK, for example, you as the buyer can be 'Gazumped'! Yes, the first time I heard this word I was wondering what my friend was talking about. In essence, even though you may sign an agreement with a buyer, if the buyer gets another, better offer while the transaction is being processed, he/she can choose to terminate the agreement with you and go with the new buyer! Unbelievable, is it not? This issue can cause a lot of uncertainty and anxiety amongst buyers and sellers. There are fortunately already talks of changing this in the future and I am sure it is a change that most UK residents would welcome. Fortunately, this problem does not apply in New Zealand.

It is always good to have your lawyer review the agreement and any special conditions before you sign it.

7. SIMPLIFIED SALES PROCESS

Similar to when you are buying a property, as a seller you also have a fairly straightforward process to complete the sales and purchase agreement, and you can then agree or disagree with any clauses the buyer wants.

If it is a buyers' market, then the buyer may have an upper hand in dictating the conditions of the agreement but if it is a sellers' market, like it has been in New Zealand for a while (during the writing of this book), then you are in a much stronger position.

Similar to the buyer, it is always good to have your lawyer review the agreement and any special conditions in it before you sign it.

8. REASONABLE MANAGEMENT FEES

In New Zealand, property management fees tend to be around 8% to 10% inclusive of GST. This includes full rental and management. This is a fair and reasonable figure. In the UK, this fee can be as high as 18%.

9. EASE OF MAINTENANCE AND ABILITY TO DIY

There are lots of tradespeople available to do maintenance of your property. You can also save a lot if you go the DIY route.

I did that for my first property and I must have saved over $5,000. And this was at a time when I was really cash strapped. In London, my wife and I saved over £2,000 by doing the bathroom works ourselves. It was a steep learning curve, but we thoroughly enjoyed it.

However, my recommendation would be to get professionals to do the work if you can afford it and/or you are uncomfortable doing the work yourself.

I, in fact, did something quite funny during the renovation of my first property. The carpet in the lounge was very old and in a bad state so we had to replace it. On inspecting the floor beneath it we found that there was actually a beautiful wooden floor that just needed some sanding and polishing. We compared the prices of re-carpeting versus rejuvenating the wooden floor and we realised that if we did the latter ourselves, it would be much cheaper and give a better outcome.

I talked to a few colleagues who knew something about this and learned the basics. I then hired a sanding machine and some safety equipment and purchased the clear varnish.

All generally went well (apart from the time my wife decided to use the sander barefoot and I almost lost it when I saw that), and we finished the whole job in a few days. Sadly, though, at the end of it all, we realised that there was a strange pattern beneath the varnish. My wife finally figured out that I had been sanding across the grain the whole time! She had even pointed this out to me in the beginning, but I told her that it was much easier to sand that way! Moral of the story — always listen to you wife! Well, it was not so bad, as we managed to survive with that floor for over five years when we finally decided to get it professionally carpeted! I now tend to listen to my wife when she gives me a tip during any DIY we do. The only exception was probably when I drilled a hole in the wall of the lounge with my beloved hammer drill and penetrated right through to our bedroom wall!

10. ABILITY TO PURCHASE IN MANY CITIES

Investors do not have to be restricted to purchasing a property within their own cities. Provided they understand the market of a target city or town, it is easy to find property through the numerous property selling websites and to manage it through a local property manager.

11. GOVERNMENT HELP FOR FIRST-TIME BUYERS

There are many government schemes for first time buyers in New Zealand. Refer to the Property Financing section later in this book.

12. AFFORDABLE INTEREST RATES

Whilst interest rates in New Zealand are not as low as they are in Europe or the US, they are still reasonable and at present are almost at all-time lows.

CURRENT TRENDS

Like every other market, the real estate market is also ever changing based on overall market dynamics, preferences of new generations, government regulation, politics, etc.

Some of the key trends in the New Zealand residential real estate market are as below:

1. Auctions and sale by negotiation rather than a price being indicated. In a market where demand exceeds supply, auctions and negotiated sales tend to be ideal ways for sellers to get the best value for their assets. There have been numerous examples in the media where the sale price of a

property at an auction far exceeded everyone's expectations. However, now that the market has dipped slightly, we may see a change in this trend.

2. Higher-density living. Given the shortage of space in Auckland, the demand exceeding supply, the government and council have been forced to allow higher-density living in certain areas through the new Unitary Plan. To this end, there are expected to be a lot more dense and multi-story housing in these areas.

3. Apartment living has become more acceptable. In the past the only people who were willing to live in apartments were students or young professionals. However, the times have changed, and apartment living is becoming more acceptable to a larger portion of the population.

4. There are some reports of younger people moving away from major cities such as Auckland, where they are priced out of the market, to other cities including smaller ones (e.g. Palmerston North) where housing is more affordable.

5. Escalating property prices have become a key part of the political agenda and different political parties have different views on how to tackle this problem. There has even been talk of reducing the offsetting of tax against mortgage interest payments — watch this space. In general, there is a huge amount of attention on stabilising or reducing property prices. A key objective of this is to avoid a major bubble burst and ensure that a large portion of the population is not deprived of home ownership. This is the case not only in New Zealand but in many countries where house prices have gone out of control in the past few years, e.g. in Canada. Now that the Labour government is in power (post 2017 election) there could be some drastic changes, including restricted foreign ownership of properties.

6. New borrowing restrictions have already been implemented order to limit speculation on properties. Property investors

need 40% deposit for a mortgage whereas owner occupiers need 20%. These rules apply nationwide. However, some exemptions apply for new builds, bridging finance, re-financing existing high Loan to Value Ratio (LVR) loans, and funding for non-routine extensive repairs due to natural disasters or weather tightness issues. Note: owner occupiers buying a second home before selling their first home are not considered investors, provided their intention is to sell the first home (www.mortgages.co.nz, 2017).

CHAPTER 19: LIFE STORIES OF OTHER PROPERTY INVESTORS

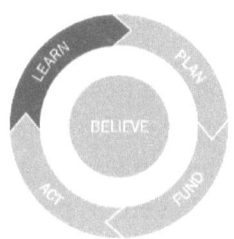

KGD, LONDON, UK

Born and raised in Melbourne, Australia with Greek ancestry.

Age: 38

When did you buy your first property?

I purchased a large three-bed Victorian terrace in Brixton Hill in October 2012 and since that time it has appreciated by 70%. I use one room and rent out the other two bedrooms to tenants who effectively service my repayments.

How did you save the deposit for the first property?

30% savings, 70% gift from family.

What challenges did you face and how did you overcome these?

I faced a number of challenges to purchase my first property in the UK, mainly around obtaining a mortgage. I arrived in the UK for the first time in August 2010 and decided I wanted to purchase a property as soon I could. This was because of the high rent and low interest rate climate, compared to Australia, where I grew up.

I was also a contractor and had no credit score, which at that time substantially limited my choice of lenders. However, I contacted a broker who led me to believe that getting a mortgage wouldn't be difficult. I therefore purchased a property, and then applied through my broker for a loan with Halifax (a bank that was favourable to contractors). But they rejected my application because I had a six-month break in employment within a year of my application. So I found myself in a situation where I had purchased a property and had no finance!

At the 11th hour I phoned another company called Contractors Financials, who brought my situation back from the brink and found a lender. There was literally only one lender in the entire country who would lend me money. It was Saffron Building Society.

Initially Saffron indicated that I would need a 20% deposit and pay a 4.95% interest. Then, probably knowing they had me *by the short and curlies*, they changed the goal posts on application time and changed the deposit requirement to 25% and the interest payment to 5.95%! My only option was to take it or continue to rent — so I took the financing.

I was fortunately able to re-mortgage the property within a year with Clydesdale Bank and my interest dropped to 3.49%. With that, I went from a complete unknown to the banks, unable to even open a bank account, to someone with a healthy credit score. So while Saffron charged me an arm and a leg in interest, they gave me a shot where other banks wouldn't and for that I am very grateful!

Did you buy any other properties or upgrade what you had?

In May 2016 I purchase a two-bed, ex-local authority flat in central Brixton at a Saville's auction. I also had a lot of fun with this purchase.

I initially thought I would obtain finance through a bank within the 20-business-day auction time scales — but I found out later that it's nigh on impossible with traditional lenders to get finance in this short timescale. I therefore had to pull out all the stops and borrow money from family to complete the transaction. Otherwise I would have lost my 10% deposit.

The Brixton investment property needed serious work and after completion of the purchase, I undertook a full refurbishment which included a new kitchen, bathroom, floors, paint and furniture. I began renting it for £2,000 per month on a 12-month AST.

I then attempted to obtain a mortgage on the unencumbered property, thinking it would be a breeze. How wrong I was! Despite the immaculate condition of the flat, its handy location close to transport and its rental at an excellent 6.5% yield, all banks in the country have refused to give me a buy-to-let mortgage on the property. This is because it is on the 7th floor of a council estate building and the private ownership level of the block is under 65%.

I purchased this property at auction for £275k. I also paid £25k for stamp duty and associated purchasing costs and £35k for a high specification refurbishment. So, as it stands, I spent a total of £335k and I've just had a sale agreed for £400k. If this falls through due to banks refusing to lend the new buyer, then I will put it on the market for cash buyers only. Failing that I will sell it through an auction. So while I don't believe I'll lose out financially with this purchase, due to the price level I purchased at auction, it has been a challenge — it has taken a lot longer than I anticipated and I've learnt a huge amount, especially about bank lending criteria and what they will and won't lend against.

I am now itching to get my capital back and move onto my next project. After much thought, my likely strategy will be to go back to the auctions, as I believe the right property can be sourced at a 25%-30% discount to market value. My strategy and advice are:

1. Purchase a small freehold period property in a growth area. Use either cash or a bridging loan.
2. Refurbish the property and let it out.
3. Get a traditional buy-to-let mortgage with a normal interest rate.
4. Extract your capital and repeat the process.

Another strategy I am keen to try out is to purchase a Household in Multiple Occupation (HMO) at the right price / location due to the high yield. According to www.gov.uk:

"A house in multiple occupation is a property rented out by at least 3 people who are not from the same 'household' (e.g. a family) but share facilities like the bathroom and kitchen."

My first house I lived in was the equivalent of a HMO and I know what young professionals want out of a property. HMOs a lot more work but I'm up for the challenge.

Any tips for budding property buyers or investors?

I would recommend picking up a number of other books for people starting their property journey. One of them is: *The*

Complete Guide to Property Investment: How to survive & thrive in the new world of buy-to-let by Rob Dix.

I've spent the last few years reading as much as I can. But the real experience and learning doesn't start until you take action — just like me buying at auction. I've learnt so much about the auction process and financing now. A few other thoughts:

- Don't be afraid to make mistakes.
- Become an expert of your local area.
- Take some risks.
- Attend property investor meetings. I found the one I attended last month quite worthwhile as it's great to be surrounded by like-minded individuals. Below are examples of property investor forums:
  - https://www.pinmeeting.co.uk/
  - https://www.propertytribes.com/ is also a fountain of knowledge. So many smart people who have already done what you want to do and on hand to provide advice.

SC, LONDON, UK

Age: 36

When did you buy your first property?

In 2004, when I was 23.

How did you save the deposit for the first property?

I sold my BMW and added it to the small bonus that I got at the time. It was £12,000 in total.

What challenges did you face and how did you overcome these?

It was a big challenge having no car for a while and having to renovate the flat with only £3,000. I also decided to buy second-hand items — for example, for the kitchen and bathroom — In order to manage the work in my very tight budget.

Did you buy any other properties or upgrade what you had?

I've upgraded to larger properties two times since my first property.

I bought a 3-bed town house in the 2008/2009 recession cheaply for £250,000. It was derelict and needed renovating. I moved in with my parents and renovated it for £3,000. I sold it 14 months later for £370,000. I didn't have another property but spent 6 months living again with my parents in 2013 while I persuaded a guy to sell me his parents' house for £450,000 rather than renting it. He eventually sold it to me and again it needed renovating, so I spent £30,000k renovating while still living with my parents.

I currently still live in the house and it has grown to a value of £660,000. We have planning permission granted to turn it from a 3-bed into a 5-bed detached family home with an estimated value of over £900,000.

Any tips for budding property buyers or investors?

Know your area where you want to buy. I always bought run-down houses in nice areas. Think schools, stations, convenience for walking etc. Look through the mess and see the potential. Ugly houses don't mean bad houses. My town house was an ugly 1970s cladded house. But it was 5 minutes' walk to the town centre and 10 minutes to the station. Additionally, the rooms were big, and the extra floor meant more space than other 'traditional' houses in the same price bracket.

TK, LONDON, UK

Age: 56

When did you buy your first property?

1995.

How did you save the deposit for the first property?

Overtime payment from my place of work and doing afterhours jobs.

What challenges did you face and how did you overcome these?

My first property was bought at the age of 27. It was a house on a barren building plot with a wire boarder fence around. The costs to hire a landscape architect were simply too much money so I did the garden layout myself. I brick-paved the open sections to improve the outside living area. The property cost and availability of money is always an issue with your first property but the more you can do yourself, the better. That way you save money, and, in the process, you'll learn a lot. Plus, you'll have a sense of "I can do it". "I did it" is a great feeling!

Did you buy any other properties or upgrade what you had?

I bought more property over the years, plus I upgraded my Windhoek property.

My first property was mortgaged. Over the years I paid extra per month to reduce the overall mortgage years. In later years, I left

Windhoek and had a tenant in the property. That way the tenant paid my monthly mortgage costs, plus I continued to pay extra monthly. In the end, I paid off a 20-year mortgage in 15 years, saving substantially on interest costs. I followed the same approach with my second residential property, with additional payments per month. After staying at this property for some time, I rented it out and the tenant basically paid my mortgage.

It is important to save some of the rental income for upgrading and general maintenance as (and when) required. I went on to buy a commercial property too. I found renting the commercial property to be much easier because of the company renting it and handling the maintenance part of it.

The discipline of saving money and managing it is key to get yourself on the property ladder. Also, I avoid borrowing money from banks for any maintenance and upgrades, in order to keep my borrowings at a manageable level, e.g. if a bathroom needs upgrading, I'll use my personal savings or the savings from the rental income to pay for it. To save on costs, I buy the material myself and use casual labour to get the job done!

My *university of life* taught me that money is a good slave, but a bad master and it is important to live within your means. Today, I own property in South Africa, Namibia and the UK.

Any tips for budding property buyers or investors?

- Location is important — so make sure you buy in the right area that has potential for growth.
- If you plan to buy and rent, make sure you target the right market. Student flats, for example, should be simplistic but modern. The less they have to maintain — i.e. garden — the better.

- Check if the property market is a buying or renting market and make your decisions accordingly.
- Make sure you have a good rental agreement in place before your tenant moves in.
- Screen the tenants before signing the lease.
- Do regular inspections of the property to see if they are taking care of the property.

DM, AUCKLAND, NEW ZEALAND

Age: 60

When did you buy your first property?

I purchased my first home at the age of 21.

How did you save the deposit for the first property?

I had a suspensory loan of $5,000 through the government. This meant that if I stayed working for them for a term, it would be paid off by the government.

What challenges did you face and how did you overcome these?

The biggest challenge, even back then, was paying the mortgage, so I got a flat mate. She paid the general expenses and I paid insurance, mortgage and rates.

Did you buy any other properties or upgrade what you had?

I was always interested in property and within 18 months I bought a section at a beach in Bay of Plenty.

I went on to marry and after just a few years I had to pay out half the value after separating with my husband. This hit me hard. However, I faced the challenge and stayed strong. I built a portfolio of 10 houses within 5 years with my new partner. The secret was to sell in Auckland and to buy in smaller towns where rental properties were in demand.

In our case, it was Oamaru, and the rent always covered the mortgages, unlike in Auckland. We sold one property in Auckland and bought three properties in Oamaru.

The big secret back then was to have everything negatively geared (i.e. where expenses were more than income), so you could save on the tax on your personal income. The benefit came from the appreciation of the property value over time.

We eventually decided to sell the properties in Oamaru and started looking for properties on the outskirts of Auckland. Our focus was to buy good investment properties. My motto was: if I wouldn't live in it, I wouldn't buy it.

Currently, we own 5 properties, but they are in much better areas than when we started, and we have chosen not to rent out one of them.

Not all of our investments have been sensible ones and we have learnt our lessons. Additionally, as time has passed, we have now decided to put more focus on helping out our children rather than further investments.

Any tips for budding property buyers or investors?

The secret, I believe, is to negotiate a good price for the property and to get a good financing deal.

Also, never put yourself at risk, and always keep your family safe by sensibly managing your finances.

I guess in hindsight I wouldn't have kept selling. That said, we are now in Mangawhai and our current property has gone up probably 5 times compared to what we paid for it 10 years ago.

IM, AUCKLAND, NEW ZEALAND

Age: 35

When did you buy your first property?

2013.

How did you save the deposit for the first property?

We had saved $12,000 over two years, we raised $5,000 from the Kiwi Saver and sold our cars and furniture for $20,000.

What challenges did you face and how did you overcome these?

I had no car for a short while, but I managed to get a beat-up old car from a friend and paid for it with the cash-back from the bank,

We bought a rundown property and had no kitchen or bathroom for 3 months. We had no money left for renovation so we started by renovating the one room we had to live in with the salary I was getting, We had to live in part of the house while I renovated the house myself with the help of family, I had to go to my parents' house to shower and cook — I mainly cooked on the deck on the barbeque.

Within 3 months I got the property re-valued, and because the value had gone up, I was able to borrow additional funds from the bank to complete the renovations. It was a rough ride for 3 months and we had to live with the bare minimum. However, it was all worth it, as I purchased the first property for $325k and within 2 years I used the equity in my first property to upgrade and buy my existing property, which is now probably worth around $1m.

Did you buy any other properties?

Yes. I bought a second property in early 2015 but had to sell the first one in order to buy it. My new property has 2 dwellings on it.

How many do you have and how did you grow your portfolio?

I got my property revalued and used the equity to upgrade to a much larger property with home and income. It was quite a challenge to buy the second property, as I was short of funds while I sold the first one. I managed to get interest-free bridging finance through friends and family. I am now in the process of building a third dwelling on the property so as to further increase the value and also to get further rental income.

Any tips for budding property buyers or investors?

- Your first home will probably never be a dream home so start with what you can afford.
- Look for properties with potential for capital gains, e.g. through improvements, growth of the area, etc.
- Talk to brokers and banks for advice. Visit your personal banker and ask questions — always seek a pre-approval.
- Show a savings history as this will help with the loan approval.
- Use government grants — the KiwiSaver, first home buyer grant, etc.
- There are now options of using parents' equity in New Zealand so make use of this if possible. You can also use gifted money for your deposit.

- If you already have existing property, get an updated valuation of it, as you may be able to use your existing equity as deposit for a new property purchase.
- Avoid personal loans, credit cards and have minimum personal debt exposure.

MP, AUCKLAND, NEW ZEALAND

Age: 52

When did you buy your first property?

I bought my first property in 1995. Incidentally, this 3-bedroom villa was later converted to fully networked office premises, which is where I first met the author of this book when he joined my company, Convergence Limited, as an analyst.

How did you save the deposit for the first property?

I borrowed from my in-laws.

What challenges did you face and how did you overcome these?

My step-father declined my request to advance NZ$10K, which represented approximately 50% of the deposit we required at the time. Hence, I had to approach my in-laws.

Did you buy any other properties or upgrade what you had?

- 1995: 3-bedroom ex-state house in One Tree Hill, Auckland – bought for $205,000, sold in 1999 for $225,000
- 1999: 3-bedroom townhouse in St Helier's, Auckland — bought for $315,000, sold in 2004 for $580,000
- 2004: 4-bedroom waterfront villa in Farm Cove, Auckland — bought for $800,000, sold in 2013 for $1.3m

- 2013: 5-bedroom clifftop house in Whangaparaoa, Auckland — bought for $1m, current value is $1.6m
- 2014: 6-bedroom rental property in Clendon Park, Auckland — bought for $430,000, current estimated value of $645,000

Any tips for budding property buyers or investors?

Try to buy and hold as much property as you can, especially in a fast and continuously growing market like Auckland, New Zealand. This is even more exaggerated by the fact that there is no capital gains tax in New Zealand, although there has been plenty of talk about changing that for the last 15 years or so. I wish I had held on to my first and second properties, which are now worth $1.3m and $1.2m respectively.

The days of buying 3-bedroom freestanding houses in Auckland for $200 to $300K are well and truly over.

Regardless, the most important piece of advice is: do it! If you can buy any property in Auckland (or any other growing city), do it.

MS, GABORONE, BOTSWANA

Age: 52

When did you buy your first property?

1991.

How did you save the deposit for the first property?

Through my personal savings since I started working in 1986.

What challenges did you face and how did you overcome these?

At the time, I had just bought my first car and I could not afford to pay property mortgage and car loans simultaneously. Fortunately, as I used the same bank for both loans, I negotiated with the bank to re-work the original car repayment plan to increase the repayment period to accommodate the mortgage repayment.

Did you buy any other properties or upgrade what you had?

I kept the first property in a very good condition and aimed to pay it off before the 20 years plan. As the property appreciated and its value increased, I removed it from the Company Housing Scheme. I used it as security to get money from the bank and bought my second property.

Any tips for budding property buyers or investors?

It is important to have goals on your savings accounts. Don't borrow money for deposits or to pay other loans. Start early, instead of paying rent for a very long time, buy early and repay the mortgages while you're still at the peak of your career life. Maintaining your property is also a *must do,* as it continuously increases the value of the property.

CHAPTER 20: TOOLS & UTILITIES

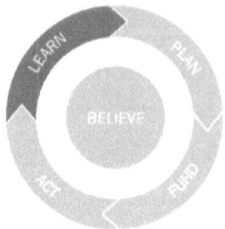

Below are some key websites, applications and utilities that can help you buy or sell a property and obtain various data on properties. These lists are not comprehensive and if you search on Google you should be able to find plenty of other tools and websites.

INFORMATIONAL WEBSITES

Below are some websites that provide data on properties. Some of these are focused on property valuations and reports, whereas others provide more general information, e.g. property values by region.

US

1. www.zillow.com — It is the leading real estate sales and rental website in the US. According to the About Us section on the website:

    "Zillow serves the full lifecycle of owning and living in a home: buying, selling, renting, financing, remodeling and more. It starts with Zillow's living database of more than 110 million U.S. homes - including homes for sale, homes for rent and homes not currently on the market, as well as Zestimate home values, Rent Zestimates and other home-

related information. Zillow operates the most popular suite of mobile real estate apps, with more than two dozen apps across all major platforms."

2. www.trulia.com – On its About Us section, it is stated that:

"At Trulia, we believe that when it comes to finding a home what's outside the front door is just as important as what's behind it. That's why we go beyond the typical listings, by sourcing insights straight from locals and offering over 34 neighborhood map overlays, to give people a deeper understanding of what living in a home and neighborhood is really like. We're committed to helping them discover a place where they will love to live and where they will feel more connected to the community and to each other. It's why we strive every day to help build a more neighborly world.

3. www.realtor.com – The website states that

"Realtor.com®, is the trusted resource for home buyers, sellers and dreamers, offering the most comprehensive database of for-sale properties, among competing national sites, and the information, tools and professional expertise to help people move confidently through every step of their home journey. It pioneered the world of digital real estate 20 years ago, and today helps make all things home simple, efficient and enjoyable. Realtor.com® is operated by News Corp subsidiary Move, Inc. under a perpetual license to operate realtor.com from the National Association of REALTORS.®"

UK

1. www.zoopla.co.uk - This is one of the best property information websites that I have ever come across in any country. You can search for house values, properties for sale, properties for rent and other information. It is very well organised and also has a great smart phone application.

2. www.rightmove.co.uk - This is another great website, which has information on property sale values, market trends, et cetera. You can also request a valuation of your property by various agents through this website. There is also a very good smart phone application for this information provider.

3. www.home.co.uk - This website provides aggregate data by postcode and regions. It can be useful for getting a sense of general prices and trends in a given area or region.

AUSTRALIA

1. www.onthehouse.com.au - The website indicates that you can search 12 million properties with estimated values, land sizes, sold histories and what's on market to buy or rent. It is a very user-friendly website and provides rich property data.

2. www.dsrdata.com.au - This is another very good website that provides property data by suburbs. The data includes vacancy rate, yield, days spent on the market and more. You can sign up for free but there are paid options for more detailed data and services.

NEW ZEALAND

1. www.oneroof.co.nz - This is a new website — a one stop shop property portal — launched in 2018. It provides property data to all parties (home owners, buyers and sellers) to make better property decisions. I have just started using it recently and am very impressed.

2. www.homes.co.nz - I also recently discovered this website and it is great to search for a property and get a rough valuation range for it at no cost.

3. www.QV.co.nz - They provide various detailed reports including electronic valuations (eValuations) but you have to pay a fee for these, e.g. a property summary report costs $49.95

4. www.terranet.co.nz - They provide various detailed reports including eValuations but you have to pay a fee for these, e.g. a property summary report costs $19.95

5. www.figure.nz - They describe themselves as a charity devoted to getting people to use data about New Zealand. They have excellent aggregate data and charts about property values by region, by type of property, etc.

GENERAL

1. www.globalpropertyguide.com - If you want to invest internationally, this website provides great information on real estate in numerous countries

PROPERTY BUYING AND SELLING WEBSITES

Below are some of the popular property buying and selling websites. These websites are not only useful for buying or selling properties, but they can give you a very good idea of market prices, trends (based on the types of properties being sold, prices, type of sale, etc.)

US

1. www.zillow.com
2. www.trulia.com
3. www.realtor.com

UK

1. www.zoopla.co.uk
2. www.rightmove.co.uk/
3. www.findproperly.co.uk/
4. www.findahood.com/
5. www.propertynetwork.net/

AUSTRALIA

1. www.domain.com.au
2. www.realestate.com.au
3. www.property.com.au
4. www.homesales.com.au
5. www.raywhite.com

NEW ZEALAND

1. www.oneroof.co.nz
2. www.trademe.co.nz
3. www.realestate.co.nz
4. www.homesell.co.nz (private sales)
5. www.harcourts.co.nz
6. www.century21global.com/for-sale-residential/New-Zealand

CHAPTER 21: CONCLUSION

I genuinely hope that you have enjoyed this book and that you have picked up at least a few important pointers from it; with any luck, a lot more.

To sum it up:

- We first learnt what real estate is and how it is valued.
- We then talked about how to get started; this included setting objectives, figuring out what, as well as where, and when to buy.
- We also covered how to determine your budget, raise funds, make an offer and complete the purchase.
- We then focused on how to move forward and manage your property, add value to it, grow your property portfolio and decide on your exit strategy.
- After that we covered some other important matters, including key pitfalls of property investment and how to avoid these, how to effectively manage your finances and how to negotiate.
- We also looked at the New Zealand real estate market as a case study to better understand the real estate dynamics of a given country or region.
- Lastly, we went through life stories of other investors and also covered some useful tools and utilities.

I wish you the best of luck in buying property, whether it is for personal or investment purposes!

APPENDIX 1

HOW TO COMPUTE COST OF EQUITY

This section is an optional read to provide a deeper understanding of how one determines the cost of equity. It is only relevant for those who are keen to learn more about how company/asset valuations work; or for curious geeks (like me)!

According to *Financial Times*, the cost of equity is the rate of return required by the company's ordinary shareholders in order for that investor to bear the risk of holding that company's shares.

You can also see from this section that these numbers are not entirely objective (i.e. there is a certain level of estimation involved), hence my earlier comment that valuations are a combination of art and science! At the end of the day, the true value of anything, including a massive asset, is what a buyer is willing to pay for it and what a seller is willing to accept for it!

$$Re = Rf + (Rm - Rf) \times \beta$$

- Re = Cost of Equity
- Rf = Risk-free rate, i.e. the return expected from investing in risk-free securities. The return on US Treasury Bills is a good proxy for this
- Rm = Market Risk Premium. This is the historic average of the excess returns that the share market has provided over and above the risk-free rate. This is estimated as 4% to 6%
- β = The volatility of the stock relative to the market. If a share price moves in line with market moves (e.g. if Anglo American's stock moves in line with FTSE) then β would be 1. If it is more volatile compared to the market, the value would be more than 1, and if it is less volatile compared to the market, the value would be less than 1.

There are companies that publish the β figures for publicly listed companies (e.g. Barra)

DISCLAIMER

The information provided within this book is for general informational purposes only. Whilst the author has endeavoured to keep the contained information up to date and correct, there are no representations or warranties, express or implied, about the completeness, accuracy, reliability, suitability or availability with respect to the information, products, services, or related graphics contained in this book for any purpose. Any use of this information is at your own risk.

A BIT MORE ABOUT ME

Sometimes I find it slightly tricky to introduce myself when I meet new people during travels or in other situations. My challenge is to explain who I am while being sincere but not sounding pretentious.

I have lived in five countries on four continents, travelled to over fifty countries and speak over seven languages, with varying levels of fluency. I am of Indian descent but was born in Africa, then lived in South America, then New Zealand, then had a small stint in France, then the UK, then Botswana, with extensive time spent in the entire region of southern Africa and now I'm back in the UK. Who knows where life will take me next!

I grew up and did my schooling in Kenya and kicked off my tertiary studies in Brazil. I eventually moved to New Zealand where I completed my degree in Computer Science with various awards. I started my career as an IT Consultant in New Zealand and then earned an MBA with distinction from the London Business School (a global Top-5 business school). After my MBA, I changed my career to focus on business strategy, finance and leading large transformational projects. I have worked in many different industries (including eight years spent in senior management in the world's oldest and largest Diamond Mining and Distribution Company) and have experience and expertise in diverse areas ranging from business strategy, innovation, finance, project management, supply chain optimisation, change management and technology.

I have run global projects with budgets of dozens of millions of dollars, delivered bottom line value of tens of millions of dollars (over US$200m in once specific case) and run large global teams. Amidst all this, I have also always had an attraction to and a penchant for real estate. Below are some of the real estate activities I have been involved in over and above my personal property investments:

1. I spent almost a year as an investment manager in an early stage real estate fund, investing in the real estate of care homes.
2. I oversaw the construction of a $20m+ extension to a state-of-the-art diamond processing building in Botswana.
3. I wrote a paper on commercial real estate service charges in the UK. This was published in the Estates Gazette in the UK and I also presented to a major industry event attended by hundreds of real estate professionals.
4. I consulted for a FTSE 100 company that is a major global real estate information provider.
5. I was co-president of the Real Estate club at London Business School.

I started my personal investments in real estate in the early 2000s and have never stopped. I started with buying ready-to-rent properties, then moved on to making improvements and extensions and have recently focused on developments. However, developments have proven far harder than I expected, particularly due to having to run them remotely from overseas! One thing I can; however, say for sure is that **life is not dull**.

My wife is French, and I met her while on a trip to Sydney. She was also there as a visitor but somehow, magically, in three months she was living with me in New Zealand. I think I spent more money on my phone bills than on rent during those three months! I still cannot believe that we actually pulled that off! Audrey is not only my wife but also my property investment partner. Although I often say "I" in this book, what I really mean in many cases is "We", as my wife and I started and built our property portfolio hand in hand. I am more of the strategist and *financial planner and she is the expert at finding us the right investments.*

I have coached and mentored numerous people both inside and outside of work. Although I am an introvert at heart, mentoring it is my passion. I get great satisfaction and joy from helping people realise their true potential. I see this book as an avenue to reach out to even more people. Even if you get one useful tip that helps you with your goals from this book, then I will have achieved my objective of writing it.